POSTCARD HISTORY SERIES

Long Island
Beaches

In 1907, seven (mostly) happy beachgoers posed on Sea Cliff Beach for photographer Henry Otto Korten (c. 1866–1915). Korten took thousands of photographs of Long Island, including many at this bathing beach is his beloved north shore village of Sea Cliff. Korten's glass-plate negatives were extensively used to produce real-photo postcards. His photographic works are important documentary sources of early 20th century Long Island. (Courtesy of Sea Cliff Village Museum: Henry Otto Korten.)

ON THE FRONT COVER: This c. 1900 real-photo postcard produced by Robert S. Feather (1861–1937) captures summer boarders enjoying a day of swimming and boating at a bathing beach fronting Stony Brook Harbor. Feather emigrated from England to the United States in 1898. He was a prolific local photographer and owned a photography business in Smithtown. (Courtesy of Three Village Historical Society.)

ON THE BACK COVER: Long Island's beaches have been shaped by the environment, recreation, and industry. This c. 1945 linen postcard was produced by Curt Teich & Company, the world's largest postcard producer, which popularized the iconic "Greetings From" format. To promote tourism in the region, the imagery featured a beach scene on the north shore and the historic Montauk Point Lighthouse on the south shore. (Courtesy of a private collection.)

POSTCARD HISTORY SERIES

Long Island Beaches

Kristen J. Nyitray

ARCADIA
PUBLISHING

Published by Arcadia Publishing
Charleston, South Carolina

Printed in the United States of America

Library of Congress Control Number: 2018966487

For all general information contact Arcadia Publishing at:
Telephone 843-853-2070
Fax 843-853-0044
E-mail sales@arcadiapublishing.com
For customer service and orders:
Toll-Free 1-888-313-2665

Visit us on the Internet at www.arcadiapublishing.com

For JP

CONTENTS

ACKNOWLEDGMENTS

My sincere gratitude is given to these individuals for sharing content, providing assistance, and granting image permissions for this book: Richard Barons, Ann M. Becker, Richard Brower, Kathleen Cash, Steven A. Czarniecki, Caroline Curtin, Martha DiVittorio, Amy Driscoll, Ellen Drucker-Albert, Regina G. Feeney, Mike Firestone, Cindy Ilardi, Amy Kasuga Folk, Edna Giffen, Julie B. Greene, Lee Gundel, Barbara Guzowski, Jaime Karbowiak, Nanette Lawrenson, Lora Lomuscio, Gary Lutz, Charles R. Mackie, Karen Martin, Andrea Meyer, Vanessa Nastro, Melissa Nuñez, Christy Orquera, Grace Palmisano, Keith Pardini, Gina Piastuck, Nancy B. Pierson, Eileen Polis, Ellen Quasha, Dave Rapelje, Sara Reres, Kerri Rosalia, Mark Rothenberg, Daniel Russ, Jennifer L. Santo, Brad C. Shupe, Geri E. Solomon, Lynn Toscano, Frank Turano, Marilyn Weigold, Andrew Wendolovske, and Caren Zatyk. Thank you to Erin Vosgien and Caitrin Cunningham at Arcadia Publishing for supportive editorial assistance. To my mother: thank you for everything.

Images in this book appear courtesy of Bayport–Blue Point Public Library (BBPPL); Bayville Historical Museum (BHM); Bellmore Memorial Library (BML); Boston Public Library (BPL); Cold Spring Harbor Library and Environmental Center (CSH); East Hampton Library, Long Island Collection (EHL); East Hampton Historical Society (EHHS); Freeport Historical Society (FHS); Glen Cove Public Library, Robert R. Coles Long Island History Collection (GLCPL); Gold Coast Public Library (GOCPL); Gold Coast Public Library and Warren and Carol Griffin, Sea Cliff, New York (GOCPL: WCG); Great Neck Library (GNL); Hicksville Public Library (HPL); Historical Society of the Massapequas (HSM); Hofstra University Libraries, Special Collections, Long Island Studies Institute (HOF); Huntington Historical Society (HHS); Library of Congress (LOC); Locust Valley Historical Society (LVHS); Mastics-Moriches-Shirley Community Library (MMSCL); Miller Place Mount Sinai Historical Society (MPMSHS); New York State Historic Newspapers (NYSHN); Patchogue-Medford Public Library (PMPL); Port Washington Public Library (PWPL); private collection (PC); Regina G. Feeney (RGF); Sea Cliff Village Museum: Henry Otto Korten (SCVM: HOK); Shelter Island Historical Society (SIHS); Southold Historical Society (SHS); Stony Brook University Libraries, Special Collections (SBU); the Bridgehampton Museum (TBM); the Historical Society of Greater Port Jefferson (THSGPJ); the Smithtown Library, Richard H. Handley Collection of Long Island Americana (TSL); Three Village Historical Society (TVHS); and Westhampton Beach Historical Society (WBHS).

INTRODUCTION

Long Island's history is uniquely intertwined with its beaches. In his poem "Starting from Paumanok," Walt Whitman described Long Island as "isle of the salty shore and breeze and brine." For millennia, wind, water, and sediments have converged to create the island's beach systems. Glacial moraines and retreats formed the distinct beach topography. North shore beaches have bluffs and characteristic glacial debris such as boulders. Kettle lakes, including Lake Ronkonkoma, were produced when significant blocks of ice thawed. The south shore and barrier islands are comprised of fine outwash sand and gravel. The earliest Native American inhabitants respected the pristine shorelines, regarding them as sacred resources that provided subsistence. Beaches were sites of whaling, fishing, and collecting clams and whelks to fashion into wampum. In the 17th century, Dutch and English settlers recognized the economic potential of beaches, which became desirable acreage for land ownership. During the American Revolution, accurate navigation of coastlines was critical for informing military tactics, maintaining the economy, and transmitting intelligence. In the late 18th century, shipwrecks caused by treacherous sea conditions, shoals, and sandbars spurred construction of lifesaving stations and lighthouses across Long Island.

In the mid- to late 19th century, beaches shifted from places fraught with potential dangers to places of respite and fresh beginnings. Long Island became a tourist haven with beaches as the lure, creating new sources of income and summer colonies. This transformative change was influenced by advances in transportation, particularly steamships and the Long Island Rail Road. An abundance of hotels and resorts were established, and countless advertisements touted the cool breezes, swimming, sailing, sportfishing, camping, picnicking, and more to be found along the shores. Ambitious real estate developers planned dozens of new communities on or near beaches. Suggestions of restorative health benefits gained from breathing salt air and swimming in pure waters were also heavily marketed. During Prohibition (1920–1933) in the United States, Long Island's beaches were the site of illegal transfers of rum and other alcohol. Throughout this period (and today), the livelihoods of resilient baymen were dependent on the original native and ancient practices of shellfishing.

In 1924, the New York State Council of Parks and the Long Island State Park Commission were founded and subsequently managed by influential planner Robert Moses, who shaped and forever changed the natural environment of Long Island. Sand dunes and pastures were transformed into parks. New roadways, causeways, and bridges linked the mainland to outer barrier islands, including Jones Beach Island and Fire Island. Moses was met with resistance from coordinated grassroot activities by local citizens. One notable example of their efforts contributed to the establishment of the Fire Island National Seashore in 1964, which thwarted Moses's intention to construct a highway across the barrier island.

Living on Long Island presents challenges, particularly for those residing in immediate coastal areas. Severe weather, including the Great New England Hurricane of 1938 (Long Island Express) and Hurricane or Superstorm Sandy in 2012 had devastating environmental and personal consequences. Dune system erosion, unprecedented flooding, and breaches (which can improve the quality of water) affected coastlines in ways still being assessed today. Homes, businesses, and personal effects were destroyed, creating hardship conditions for many Long Islanders.

Researching Long Island's beaches, locating vintage postcards to document them, and writing about how the imagery reflects history was an intensive experience. At the outset, five key questions needed to be addressed. First, how does one define a beach? I drew upon scientific specifications, including geomorphic features to inform the scope of what constitutes a "beach." I also chose to cast a large net, relying on Merriam-Webster's definition of "a shore of a body of water covered by sand, gravel, or larger rock fragments." In addition to oceans and bays, beaches can be found along rivers, lagoons, ponds, inlets, coves, and lakes. Second, how does one define Long Island? In this book, it is Nassau and Suffolk Counties. The geography includes Brooklyn and Queens; however, excellent books specifically focused on beaches within the borough of New York City are available from Arcadia Publishing. Third, how should the content be organized, considering beaches can be found among two counties, multiple shorelines, barrier islands, a lake, two forks, and an island situated between the forks? The chapters are arranged by county, then by shore (north and south), and then alphabetized by community. Chapter three, titled "Central Shores," includes Lake Ronkonkoma and Shelter Island. The fourth question was: from where could postcards be obtained? Through extensive research, content was located and most requests made to libraries, cultural institutions, and private collectors were met with enthusiasm and fulfilled. And finally, where could a master list of beaches within Nassau and Suffolk Counties be found? The answer is: one did not exist. This book project required creating an inventory, which proved to be a complex process considering Long Island has beaches owned and managed by state, county, city, town, village, hamlet, and private entities.

Postcards are visual culture that document and communicate points of view, social norms, and history. The golden age of postcards was 1907 to 1915, and beaches are a popular subject found pictured on them. However, it is important to recognize that many Long Island scenes and residents are not represented in these ephemeral sources. Economic, religious, and racial prejudices impacted access to beaches; if you did not own one or belong to a beach club, admittance was limited. The development of town and state parks would mitigate this issue with time. However, archival silences and gaps exist, as postcards depicting diverse populations across Long Island were not found. For example, African Americans held annual celebrations at Hemlock Beach south of mainland Amityville from 1841 to 1910, and between 1947 and 1961, they founded three beach communities in Sag Harbor: Azurest, Sag Harbor Hills, and Nineveh. Postcards documenting these histories are nonexistent.

Great effort was made to present a variety of beaches on Long Island. In conformity with space guidelines, not all beaches could be included in the book. Conversely, postcards were not produced for many beaches. A small percentage of maps, photographs, and manuscripts were allowed and selected to supplement the postcards. Also, a few scarce images were identified and desired for inclusion, but the financial costs of obtaining them and securing publishing rights were simply too prohibitive.

In addition to the titles listed in the bibliography, numerous print and electronic resources were consulted. Recommended sources for further study include Brooklyn Newsstand (bklyn. newspapers.com), HathiTrust Digital Library (hathitrust.org), MetroPostcard (metropostcard. com), New York Heritage Digital Collections (nyheritage.org), New York State Historic Newspapers (nyshistoricnewspapers.org), Old Fulton New York Postcards (fultonsearch.org), and Arcadia Publishing's titles on Long Island.

Today, technology has reimagined traditional postcards as Instagram and Facebook posts. However, the premise of forming social connections by sharing brief, written personal sentiments coupled with images remains unchanged.

Royalties from the sale of this book will be donated to organizations that steward Long Island historical collections and beaches. My highest respects and regards are given to individuals who dedicate time to these important and worthy endeavors that ensure our connections to the past are preserved.

One

NASSAU COUNTY, NORTH SHORE BEACHES

Through poetry and artistry, this c. 1908 postcard extols the splendors of Long Island's beaches. "Here's to the Queen of most beautiful Isles . . . Whose shores are kissed by the ocean's sweet mouth / Whose breezes whisper of vigor and health. / Where boating, and hunting, and fishing abound, / Where the merriest crowd of bathers is found; / For home and pleasure she stands above all, / Here's to Long Island the best of all." (PC.)

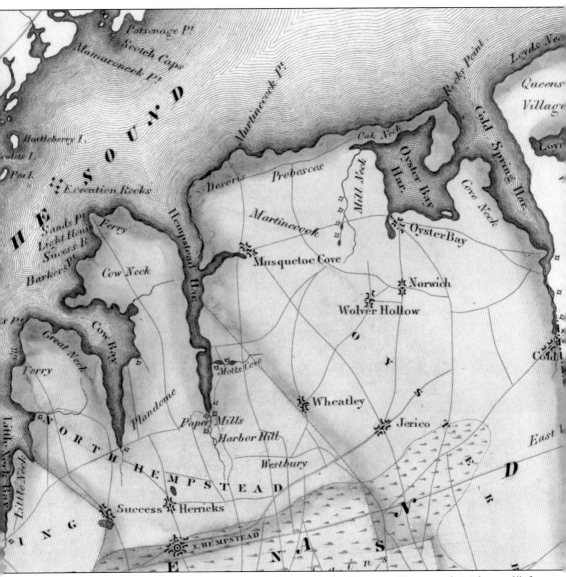

This section of "Map of the Counties of New York, Queens, Kings, and Richmond" from David H. Burr's *An Atlas of the State of New York, Containing a Map of the State and of the Several Counties* (1829) depicts the north shore geography and communities situated on Long Island Sound in the townships of North Hempstead and Oyster Bay. These towns seceded from Queens County in 1899 with the establishment of Nassau County. Over time, the names of several communities and bodies of water have changed, including Probasco (Lattingtown) and Oak Neck (Bayville). Cow Bay, situated between Great Neck and Manhasset, is known today as Manhasset Harbor. In the late 19th century, these coastal areas evolved into popular resort destinations, particularly among New York City residents seeking relief from the summer heat. Easy access to beachfront areas on the north shore was afforded by ferry service, rail transportation, and stagecoach. (SBU.)

Located between Lattington and Centre Island is the village of Bayville. Several beaches encompass the community, including Soundside Beach Park, Stehli Beach, Centre Island Beach, West Harbor Beach Memorial Park, and Bayville Beach. The Bayville Casino, near Charles E. Ransom Beach, was built in 1913 and first owned by real estate developer Zebulon Wilson (1870–1937). It was a popular venue for dining, dancing, movies, skating, and bowling. In the photograph above, employees of the Wetterauer Dress Factory of Hicksville posed on the sand by the casino during a company outing. The c. 1921 postcard below documents the casino and beach two years before the building was destroyed by a fire. (Above, HPL; below, BHM.)

The Casino and Beach.   Oyster Bay, L. I.

Centre Island, L. I.

On the Way to Huntington L. J. Charles

Centre Island is surrounded by four miles of coastline fronting Cold Spring Harbor, Oyster Bay Harbor, and Long Island Sound. Glacial till formed the beaches on the peninsula. In the early 1900s, bungalow residences were located on Centre Island Beach at eastern Bayville. This c. 1905 postcard shows a bird's-eye view of a waterfront residence known as The Folly, commissioned by George Bullock and designed by the architectural firm Renwick, Aspinwall & Owen. (HOF.)

1632   HARBOR BEACH PAVILION, GLEN COVE L. I.   ILLUSTRATED POST CARD CO., N. Y.

The Harbor Beach Association of Glen Cove formed in 1902 to ensure local residents would have beach access. Private land ownership prevented admittance to Hempstead Harbor, and the association successfully negotiated a lease with landowner John Appleby. This c. 1906 postcard shows the Harbor Beach Pavilion. Designed by William T. Lawson, it was built with funds raised by the association. By 1922, the building was no longer in use. (LVHS.)

IN THE WATER AT GLEN COVE, LONG ISLAND, N. Y.

The city of Glen Cove is home to Pryibil Beach, Crescent Beach, and Morgan Park. In the early 1900s, several of the country's wealthiest industrialists and business executives maintained residences on Glen Cove's coastline, including the benefactor of Morgan Memorial Park, John Pierpont Morgan Jr. (1867–1943). Morgan purchased land to create a park on Hempstead Harbor at a cost of $1 million. Created in honor of his late wife, Jane, he gifted the park to the people of Glen Cove and Locust Valley. *The New York Times* reported on May 27, 1926: "Gift breaks chain of private estates on seven-mile waterfront, gives public access to Sound." Designed by architects Charles Leavitt & Son, the recreational facility and beach were engineered to be child friendly with sheltered and shallow bathing areas. It formally opened on July 17, 1932. (Both, GLCPL.)

MORGAN BEACH - GLEN COVE, N.Y.

KARATSONYI'S HOTEL, GLENWOOD, L.I.

Located 25 miles from New York City and overlooking Hempstead Harbor was the impressive north shore resort known at various times as Glenwood Hotel, Hotel Glenwood-Hungaria, and Karatsonyi's Hotel. The 27-acre complex was founded in 1892 on the former James Mott estate. Business partners and proprietors Nicholas Karatsonyi (c. 1850–1929) and Adolph G. Kmetz (1858–1918) marketed the hotel's "luxuries and comforts of city life amidst beautiful country surroundings" and its "perfect beaches." The venue hosted company retreats, corporate meetings, and political fundraisers. Advertisements emphasized its easy accessibility from New York City, including by scenic car drives and the Long Island Rail Road. The Long Island Sound steamers *Nantasket*, *Crescent*, and *Sagamore* were also utilized as the resort had a dock. In December 1911, the hotel was destroyed by a fire, but it was later rebuilt. (GOCPL.)

Bathing Glenwood, L.I.

Karatsonyi's Hotel offered a wide spectrum of amenities and activities for health, rest, and recreation, including beach bathing, baseball fields, fishing, boating, yachting, and fine dining. This c. 1912 oversized postcard shows two scenes of the beach area with a pier, a bathhouse, and swimmers. Verandas provided expansive views of Hempstead Harbor. The resort served as a venue for diverse gatherings, even becoming a temporary base for the 1905 and 1906 Vanderbilt Cup Race–winning French Darracq team. Gradually, a shift in tourist interests occurred with the expansion of the New York state park system. Increased access to beaches coupled with Nicholas Karatsonyi's death in 1929 contributed to the demise of the resort. In 1947, the Long Island Lighting Company purchased the hotel and acreage to construct a gas manufacturing plant for the rapidly growing population of Nassau County. The hotel was subsequently razed. (GOCPL: WCG.)

BATHING PAVILION, GREAT NECK, L. I. N. Y.

Great Neck is comprised of nine villages and encompasses a peninsula surrounded by Little Neck Bay and Manhasset Bay. In 1927, Louise Eldridge (1860–1947) assumed her late husband's mayoral position in Saddle Rock, becoming the first female mayor in New York. The Eldridges helped found the public library, a park district, and the public beach pictured on this c. 1928 postcard at the former site of Hayden's Coal Yard. (HOF.)

STEPPING STONE BEACH, GREAT NECK, N.Y.

Steppingstone Park and Beach in Kings Point is part of the Great Neck Park District. Located on Long Island Sound, the land was previously owned by luxury retailer Henri Bendel (1868–1936) and later Walter Chrysler (1875–1940), founder of the automobile corporation. During World War II, the original beach area was shifted to this location because the grounds were needed to establish the United States Merchant Marine Academy. (GNL.)

These two postcards feature shore scenes of sailing, bathing, and wading in Oyster Bay waters. In 1941, the Beekman Family Association deeded beachfront land in Oyster Bay to the town. Today, Beekman Beach functions as a passive park. Improvements have been made to the overlook with funds privately raised by the Oyster Bay Lions Club. In 1928, the Theodore Roosevelt Memorial Park and Beach was dedicated, and in 1942, the Theodore Roosevelt Association gifted the property to the Town of Oyster Bay. Stewardship of beaches is critical to sustaining Long Island's natural habitat and maintaining environmental health. Working with local government agencies, The Friends of the Bay monitor the quality of Oyster Bay and Cold Spring Harbor waters and advocate for the preservation and restoration of these areas. (Above, LVHS; below, PC.)

A bit of the Shore, Oyster Bay, L. I.

This c. 1906 photograph shows bathers swimming and playing in the water at Ryder's Bathing Beach in Port Washington. Located near Shore Road and Second Avenue, the popular venue had an area where guests could swim and rent rowboats. The white changing cabana had the word "Bathing" prominently displayed on it. Each letter and the two end sections functioned as small, individual changing rooms. (PWPL.)

Beginning in the late 1890s, Long Island's north shore Gold Coast, with its many inlets and deep bays, became a destination for high society's social and nautical activities. This bathing beach in Port Washington was located on the site of present-day Port Washington Yacht Club. The postcard depicts a woman and children wading by the original clubhouse. (PC.)

Plain Talk

Vol. II, No. 18.   PORT WASHINGTON, N. Y., AUGUST 31, 1912   5 Cents Per Copy
$1.00 Per Year

COME IN—
THE WATER'S FINE.

Plain Talk magazine was published from 1911 to 1914. Targeted to Port Washington and north shore residents, it circulated every Saturday. Contents included articles on local politics, real estate developments, transportation issues, and social events, along with business advertisements. It is a trove of original source information for research on early-20th-century Long Island. The pictured issue was published on August 31, 1912, and includes an impassioned editorial by Henry Kuizer Landis on the topic of beaches. Advocating for the establishment of a publicly accessible beach, he wrote, "There will be children learning to swim ten years and a generation from now—let us give them the opportunity. Although three yacht club beaches are in use . . . we have an excellent opportunity to make a bathing beach. Why not do it?" (PWPL.)

BAR BEACH, TOWN OF NORTH HEMPSTEAD, LONG ISLAND, N.Y.

These two c. 1952 postcards produced by Tomlin Greeting Card Company of Northport, New York, capture summer scenes at Bar Beach on the western shore of Hempstead Harbor. Photographer Milton Price and wife Muriel Price's postcard business was well known for its collotype picture or "natural view" images. Tomlin (an anagram of Milton) published more than 8,000 unique cards from Milton Price's own high-quality negatives. The card above is looking east toward Glenwood Landing and Sea Cliff. In 1908 and 1912, the Town of North Hempstead's ownership of Bar Beach was reaffirmed in court decisions. Title to the beach was traced to a 1664 colonial patent. Today, this area is part of North Hempstead Beach Park. (Above, GOCPL; below, PC.)

BAR BEACH, TOWN OF NORTH HEMPSTEAD, LONG ISLAND, N.Y.

Mott's Point was an independent enclave until becoming part of the village of Sands Point in 1917. Four bathers are pictured at Mott's Point in 1911 on the coarse gravel beach, ready to swim at the water's edge. Sea Cliff and Glen Cove can be seen in the distance. In the early 1900s, many regattas were held in Hempstead Bay, and yachts sailed past buoys at Mott's Point. (PWPL.)

Sands Point Beach Hotel on Long Island Sound, opposite Glen Island, was owned by proprietors John Koch and T.C. Yauman. An on-site steamboat landing welcomed guests arriving from Peck Slip and Thirty-First Street in Manhattan. This c. 1884 artistic rendering depicts a sweeping view of the seven-acre summer resort that offered guests bathing, fishing, and boating. The hotel was destroyed by fire on October 23, 1892. (PWPL.)

The Beach, Sea Cliff, L. I.

The historic village of Sea Cliff is situated between Glenwood Landing and Glen Cove. Views from the steep bluffs present expansive vistas of Hempstead Harbor and Long Island Sound. *The New York Times* declared Sea Cliff a favorite summer destination on May 30, 1897. The community was touted for its picturesque surroundings and for its beach bathing described as "not only convenient and pleasant but absolutely safe." The c. 1904 postcard above and the photograph below capture spirited summer days at the beach complete with swimming, boating, and strolling along the boardwalk. Today, residents can access and enjoy several beaches, including nearby Harry Tappen Beach and Sea Cliff Municipal Beach. (Above, HOF; below, SCVM: HOK.

Titled "Bathing Girls at Edgewater Beach," these c. 1907 photographs were taken in Sea Cliff by Henry Otto Korten (c. 1866–1915). After completing coursework in the arts at Cooper Union, Korten found success as a salesman for the Illustrated Postcard and Novelty Company. He pursued artistic endeavors and took thousands of photographs of Long Island, including beaches. Using his collection of glass-plate negatives, Korten produced and sold his prints and postcards. He resided in Sea Cliff with his family from 1901 until his death in 1915. Edgewater Pavilion, seen in the photograph below, was owned by Phebe Campbell. It was advertised as "the coolest spot on the beach and a delightful family resort where afternoons and evenings may be enjoyed with all modern conveniences." The pavilion was destroyed by a fire in April 1907 while undergoing renovations. (Both, SCVM: HOK.)

June 17 1905

1752

PANORAMA OF SE

Where we went on a

Enjoyment of Long Island beachfronts was not limited to warm summertime months. This c. 1905 panoramic postcard illustrates a winter scene in Sea Cliff. Pictured in the foreground are women and children ice skating and standing on frozen Hempstead Harbor. Located on the high bluffs in the background are houses in Sands Point. Several boats are clustered near the shore. Advances in photography allowed wide landscape scenes to be captured and printed in

IN WINTER.

ILL. POST CARD CO., N. Y.

an oversized format. In 1904, the Cirkut Panoramic Outfit camera was patented, which could rotate 360 degrees. This feature enabled photographers to show the full expanse of a subject, typically scenery or a group of people. Double-width postcards such as this one are two to eight times the length of standard cards and were typically folded to minimize additional postage fees. (HOF.)

5285   BATHING AT TILLEY'S, SEA CLIFF, L.I.

Camping out in Glenwood Landg about 2½ miles fr
Have a fine time   here.   Robert.

Pathway to the Shore, Sea Cliff, L.I.

From the late 1880s to the early 1900s, Tilley's beach and pavilion were popular gathering spots in Sea Cliff for recreational and social activities. Many of the grand Victorian houses and quaint Craftsman-style bungalows for which the village is known were built high on the bluffs (one is pictured at top in the above image). These homes had convenient access to the beach along with optimal views of Hempstead Harbor and Long Island Sound. (PC.)

Two women and a child walk down a tree-lined pathway in Sea Cliff toward the shores of Hempstead Harbor in this c. 1908 postcard. Nearly a dozen walkways and stairways, some quite steep, provided access from the bluffs to the beach. With time, railings and steps became structurally compromised from storm damage and age. The Sea Cliff Landmarks Association and village government are working to restore these historic structures. (HOF.)

Two

NASSAU COUNTY, SOUTH SHORE BEACHES

Poster stamps touting Nassau County as the "Glamour Land of Ocean Sport" were published during the 1939–1940 New York World's Fair. The circular graphic on the left depicts the Trylon and Perisphere structures at the futuristic-themed exposition. It included the phrase "6 miles to," which highlighted the short distance between the venue at Flushing Meadows–Corona Park in Queens and the beaches in Nassau County. (PC.)

LONG ISLAND'S
SOUTH SHORE

from

Atlantic Beach to Montauk Point

PRESENTS 100 MILES OF HOME COMMUNITIES

⟨≫⟩

A **GREAT** place to live, with comfortable homes and modern conveniences, broad highways, protected waterways, vast recreational parks and clean ocean beaches, with commuters' express train service to Manhattan, Brooklyn and Queens.

⟨≫⟩

Your own particular questions as to the features of the various communities will be answered by

THE SECRETARY

SUNRISERS OF LONG ISLAND, Inc.

⟨≫⟩ *A Division of the Long Island Chamber of Commerce* ⟨≫⟩

TELEPHONE PENNSYLVANIA 2190

20 WEST 34TH STREET   NEW YORK CITY

Beginning in the mid- to late 19th century, the Long Island Rail Road, ambitious real estate developers, and the Long Island Chamber of Commerce produced a wide spectrum of travel and description guidebooks to attract potential homebuyers to the suburbs and to bolster tourism. In these promotional publications, the island was marketed for its untapped economic potential, the healthy lifestyle it afforded, and the region's close proximity to New York City. Many advertisements focused on the allure of the beaches. In the 1929 edition of *Long Island: The Sunrise Home Land*, this full-page advertisement announced "Long Island's South Shore from Atlantic Beach to Montauk Point Presents 100 Miles of Home Communities." Long Island was characterized as "a great place to live with comfortable homes and modern conveniences, broad highways, vast recreational parks and clean ocean beaches with commuters' express train service to Manhattan, Brooklyn and Queens." (SBU.)

NAUTILUS BEACH CLUB
Atlantic Beach, N. Y.

487

Atlantic Beach is located at the western end of Long Beach Barrier Island, four miles east of Queens County. In 1923, banker Stephen P. Pettit of Freeport founded Atlantic Beach Associates. Pettit sought to transform the sand dunes that comprised Atlantic Beach into a residential community and resort destination. With aspirations to exceed the success of neighboring Long Beach, he spent $1 million to prepare the land, but died before work was completed. His vision was re-sparked three years later by developer William L. Austin, who led Island Park Associates and acquired the acreage for a reported $5 million. Construction of a bridge over Reynolds Channel in 1927 connected Far Rockaway and Atlantic Beach. The Nautilus Hotel and Beach Club, pictured on this c. 1936 postcard, opened in 1930 with much fanfare. Described as ritzy, the site featured a private 500-foot beach, 240 rooms, and a large cabana. Rooms were later converted to apartments and marketed for their direct access to the rolling surf and the "opportunity to live quietly, spaciously, and in complete relaxation." (PC.)

This c. 1940 postcard provides an aerial view of the Nautilus Hotel and Beach Club in Atlantic Beach. The Atlantic Ocean is at bottom right. A fire destroyed the hotel in 1960. The loss was stated to have affected navigation on the sea, as boats and ships could no longer reference the visual landmark. (HOF.)

Surf Club, Atlantic Beach, Long Island, New York (Beach scene III) is a c. 1947 photograph credited to the photography firm of Gottscho-Schleisner Inc. Samuel H. Gottscho (1875–1971) and his son-in-law William H. Schleisner (1912–1962) documented nature, social life, and architecture, primarily from New York to Florida. Real estate developer William L. Austin founded the pictured Sun and Surf Club and the Silver Point Beach Club at Atlantic Beach. (LOC.)

The SURFSIDE — ATLANTIC BEACH — L. I.   7A-H1812

The New York Times positively reviewed The Surfside for its airy "Hollywood" design aesthetic and its novel business model in the June 5, 1937, edition. Located on Brookline Avenue in Atlantic Beach, the venue functioned as a casino, club, and bathing beach. For a flat fee of $3, guests could enjoy the beach, swimming pool, dinner, dancing, and entertainment. This postcard is a C.T. Art Colortone full color card, which is a five-color process produced on linen finish stock by Curt Teich & Company of Chicago. The written comments on this postcard state: "This has been a delightful day. Bathing on the private beach, smart exclusive atmosphere and now enjoying the wonderful food." (Both, HOF.)

Freeport was settled in the mid-17th century as Great South Woods and later renamed Raynor South and Raynortown after a founding family. Incorporated as a village in 1892, the accessibility to streams, canals, Great South Bay, and the Atlantic supported maritime industries. In the late 19th century, improvements in transportation spurred Freeport's development as a resort community and summer destination, particularly with actors, artists, and writers from New York City. In the northern section of Woodcleft Canal was Freeport Bathing Beach. It had a shorefront pavilion that provided a place to prepare for swims and sails. The *Brooklyn Daily Eagle* announced on May 21, 1936, the seasonal opening of beaches in Freeport, which included Beau Rivage, Playland Pool, Casino Pool, and Meister Beach. (Above, HOF; below, FHS.)

This c. 1910 photograph of a two-story, elevated stilt beach house raised on piles was taken in the vicinity of Freeport. Several people are pictured standing and sitting on the porch. While the stilts gave some protection against rising waters, the beachfront residences were highly susceptible to damage from storm surges and hurricanes. (FHS.)

Woodcleft Beach and Canal, Freeport, L. I.

This c. 1914 postcard shows the north end of Woodcleft Beach and Canal with moored boats and homes to the west. John J. Randall and William G. Miller created a Venice-inspired canal and a beach community of homes for year-round residency "not excelled in size and architectural beauty anywhere within the Greater New York." The associated Woodcleft Inn was promoted for its excellent surf and still-water bathing. (FHS.)

The photograph above captures a scene of boats sailing on choppy waters in Randall Bay. The South Shore Yacht Club is to the left, and the Freeport Casino, Bathing Beach, and Pool can be seen in the background at right. The c. 1915 postcard below of the latter venue (the former Norwood Hotel and Anchorage) shows the popularity of the beach on Casino Avenue, located north of Randall Bay. Built in 1908 by John G. Randall, it housed a restaurant and hosted thousands of visitors. A fire destroyed the original building in January 1929; however, beach bathing was still accessible, and the pool complex remained open through 1976. (Both, FHS.)

LIDO CLUB HOTEL, LONG BEACH, LONG ISLAND, N.Y.

The opulent oceanfront Lido Club Hotel opened in Lido Beach to much excitement on June 17, 1929. Featuring Moorish architecture with a pink exterior, the hotel was built at a cost of $4 million by Long Beach developer and New York state senator William H. Reynolds (1867–1931). Influenced by the finest hotels on the French Riviera and in Miami, amenities included surf bathing on a private beach, golf, and tennis. After Reynolds's death, the property changed ownership several times. During World War II, the US Navy used the building as a training and discharge station. It also functioned as a school and as a hospital before eventually being converted to a condominium complex in 1981. (Above, PC; below, HOF.)

U. S. Naval Receiving Station,
Lido Beach, Long Island, New York

3 LBA
U. S. Navy Official Photo

PRIVATE BEACH
NO TRESPASSING

The city of Long Beach is situated between Atlantic Beach and Lido Beach. In the late 19th century, Austin Corbin (1827–1896) founded the Long Beach Hotel and established rail transportation in partnership with the Long Island Rail Road. Real estate mogul William H. Reynolds later formulated an ambitious vision for "The City by the Sea." By the age of 40, Reynolds was a highly successful developer, with Coney Island's Dreamland amusement park and several neighborhoods in Brooklyn to his credit. In January 1907, *The New York Times* announced that the Long Beach Development Company, with Reynolds as president, planned to create a 2,000-acre city with beachfront hotels, a boardwalk, and entertainment venues. An advertisement published in May 1907 boldly declared that Long Beach was "destined to become the most famous in the world." (Left, PC; below, BPL.)

Greetings from Long Beach Long Island, N. Y.

69435

125

The Tennis Court *c. Z. Reds.* Long Beach, L. I.

Extraordinary dredging projects created the land needed to develop the city of Long Beach. An account published on December 5, 1907, in the *Brooklyn Daily Eagle* stated that the magnitude of work was second only to the Panama Canal. Twenty-four-hour operations widened the channel named after William H. Reynolds, filled marshes, and transformed the sandbar into elevated acreage. Scenic bridges and causeways connected Long Beach Barrier Island with the mainland and provided access for automobiles. The c. 1934 aerial photograph below documents the construction of Reynolds Channel Causeway or Long Beach Loop Parkway. Robert Moses's plan to link New York parks advanced when an exchange was completed at the Meadowbrook Parkway and Loop Parkway terminating at Point Lookout. (Above, SBU; below, HOF.)

Real estate developer William H. Reynolds promoted Long Beach as having the finest stretch of beach on the Atlantic Seaboard. In anticipation of opening the 300-room Hotel Nassau (right) in June 1909, advertisements highlighted its offerings of first-class services and food as expected from a luxury New York hotel. The building was fireproof and had both hot and cool saltwater and freshwater in all bathrooms. Activities included surf bathing in the ocean and dining along the boardwalk. The 400-foot frontage provided beachgoers ample room to settle on the sand and enjoy the views. The National Bathing Pavilion (left) was founded in 1908 at a cost of $100,000. Unfortunately, it was destroyed by a fire in 1913. This photograph and real-photo postcard were produced by Ambrose Fowler (c. 1844–1916). Fowler worked as an official photographer for Columbia University and specialized in photography of architectural views, groups, and fine interiors. (PC.)

This early-20th-century real-photo postcard by Ambrose Fowler documents the popularity of the Long Beach boardwalk. The view looking east includes the Hotel Nassau on the left or north and the Atlantic Ocean beach on the right or south. An advertisement published in *The New York Times* on April 10, 1909, summarized the essence of the locale: "Two years ago, Long Beach was a dream—an idea. But it has come true—the castle has materialized into the fondly dreamed-of Atlantic City for New York. Today you can go to Long Beach and see a beautiful seaside city springing up on what was once barren 2400 acre waste of sand. The sight is one to inspire. The great $680,000 boardwalk, the imposing $750,000 hotel, the wonderful Casino, the maze of beautiful villas, the famous beach and—well, you must see it all to appreciate it." Long Beach became a city in 1922. William H. Reynolds served as its first mayor. (PC.)

This elevated or bird's-eye view rendering shows the expansive oceanfront boardwalk in Long Beach. For developer William H. Reynolds, the walkway was the heart and anchor of his "Riviera of the East." Newspaper articles published in October 1907 describe elephant labor aiding in construction of the boardwalk. Reports stated elephants Alice and Roger were procured from Bombay and briefly used to lift timber and pull train cars filled with stone for the concrete pilings and foundation. By June 1908, two miles of the boardwalk were completed, and it became the place where recreation, tourism, and commerce converged. It also drew people seeking health benefits through walking the expanse and breathing in the salt air, which was a suggested therapy for a myriad of conditions. In September 2012, Long Beach was devastated by Hurricane Sandy, and the boardwalk sustained irreparable damage. The resilient city held a ceremony in January 2013 to commemorate the historical significance of the structure and to mark rebuilding efforts. A new 2.2-mile boardwalk opened on October 25, 2013, with entrances between Nevada Avenue and Pacific Boulevard. (HOF.)

Founded in 1958, the Green Harbor Beach Club on the Great South Bay in Massapequa is a private club; however, membership is available to nonresidents. This photograph of the club was taken in 1962. The Philip B. Healey Beach at Florence Avenue and the Biltmore Beach Club are also located in Massapequa. (HSM.)

TOBAY BEACH
TOWN OF OYSTER BAY
PROPOSED EXPANSION OF FACILITIES

Supervisor _____

John J Burns

This c. 1958 rendering is a plan for Tobay Beach. The proposal included an inland dock, a 17,000-foot expanded bathing beach, and a boardwalk. In 1960, a $750,000 project added a marina, pavilion, and parking for 5,000 cars. Tobay, an acronym for town of Oyster Bay, is between Jones Beach State Park to the west and Gilgo Beach to the east. (HOF.)

This postcard, mailed in August 1908, features visitors traveling by ferry from Freeport to Nassau-by-the-Sea (at Point Lookout Beach), the most eastern part of Long Beach Barrier Island. The trip took approximately 1.5 hours. By the early 1900s, demand for bungalows and cottages in this locale had markedly increased, and developers responded by investing heavily in construction and infrastructure projects. In 1904, the Nassau Cottage and Realty Company of Hempstead began work on the summer colony it named Nassau-by-the-Sea. An advertisement published in the July 6, 1907, *Brooklyn Daily Eagle* proclaimed Nassau-by-the Sea had "the greatest beach in the world." The sender of this postcard wrote, "On our annual S.S. beach party tomorrow (12th) to High Hill Beach. Would have been pleased to have had you along." (Both, FHS.)

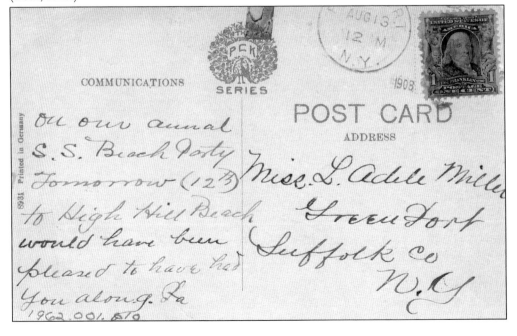

On the most eastern part of Long Beach Barrier Island is the hamlet of Point Lookout. This area was the site of the Long Beach East End Station or Station Point Lookout, New York, which was established around 1853. The c. 1907 postcard above depicts the building in Point Lookout as it appeared in the 1870s. In 1888, there were 32 station keepers across Long Island. Capt. Andrew Rhodes was the keeper here from 1880 to 1902. The US Life-Saving Service was founded in 1848 and merged with the US Revenue Cutter Service to form the US Coast Guard in 1915. The station was decommissioned after World War II, and in 1947, the property was acquired and transformed by the Point Lookout Community Church. In 2016, a grassroots fundraising campaign led by the Point Lookout Civic Association restored the station's historic flag tower. (Above, FHS; below, RGF.)

LIFE SAVERS TO THE RESCUE, POINT LOOKOUT STATION. FREEPORT, L. I.

Ellisons Hotel, Point Lookout, Freeport, L. I.

Imported and Published
by The Freeport Souvenir Post Card Co.,
Freeport, L.I.

In the early 1900s, the Long Beach Transportation Company operated a ferry steamer service from Freeport to Point Lookout. Once at Point Lookout, guests could stay overnight on the beach at the 25-room Ellison's Hotel, pictured in the postcard above. Brothers Gordon P. Ellison and Willet C. Ellison were proprietors of several beachfront establishments along the south shore. This hotel was built amidst sand dunes and beach grass and was a popular destination for large gatherings, music concerts, and dancing. Several people are pictured standing on the hotel's wide wraparound porch. The postcard below provides a scenic view of Point Lookout Beach. Several people are gathered on the beach, along with two men standing in the foreground by a lifeguard boat. (Above, FHS; below, HOF.)

Point Lookout Beach, Point Lookout, N. Y.

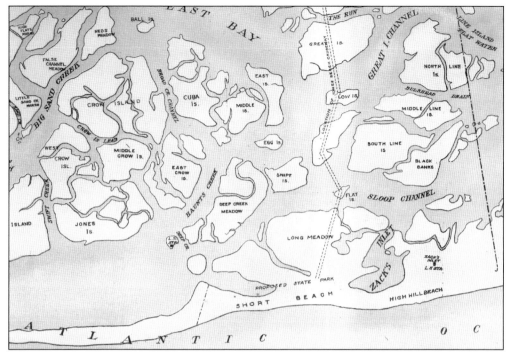

This scarce *Real Estate Reference Map of Nassau County, Long Island* by E. Belcher Hyde was published in 1927 and includes notation of "Short Beach," "High Hill Beach," and a "proposed state park" (Jones Beach State Park). At this time, Jones Beach Island was only accessible by boat. The double dotted line marked the prospective Jones Beach Causeway, intended to create unprecedented public access to south shore ocean beaches. (SBU.)

In anticipation of establishing Jones Beach State Park, master builder Robert Moses (1888–1981) declared in April 1928: "Construction of the Jones Beach Causeway is one of the most important projects ever conceived for the development of the South Shore of Long Island." Engineering of the five-mile causeway to connect Merrick Road in Wantagh over the Great South Bay to Jones Beach Island was underway in winter 1928. (HOF.)

COTTAGES AND
BOARDWALD
HIGH HILL BEACH N.Y.

High Hill Beach was located between the Atlantic and the shore of Zach's Bay. The area is now part of Jones Beach State Park. Early on, baymen made their livelihoods at this beach by hunting, clamming, fishing, and harvesting salt hay. The summer colony at High Hill existed from about 1897 to 1940. It was a self-sufficient community and vacation destination with nearly 100 buildings, including a lifesaving station, a post office, a general store, and Savage's Hotel and Cottages. A Robert Moses–influenced eviction mandate was later enforced when the Town of Hempstead transferred land by conveyance to New York State. Moses's vision for a new state park did not include a residential enclave. By 1940, nearly 60 of the remaining homes at High Hill were relocated four miles east to West Gilgo Beach. (Both, HOF.)

Looking South from Savage's Hotel.   High Hill Beach, L. I.

After years of calculated planning by Robert Moses, Jones Beach State Park and the causeway were dedicated and opened on August 4, 1929. Moses's ambitious, holistic design provided unparalleled access to south shore beaches and was made possible by executing complex engineering feats and reconfiguring the natural landscape. Located 20 miles from New York City, the park is comprised of 2,400 acres situated between the Atlantic Ocean and the Great South Bay on Jones Beach Island. In 1933, the Long Island State Commission published this illustrated booklet distributed by Jones Beach Shops to promote the park. Both the island and the park are named after the Irish-born Maj. Thomas Jones (c. 1665–1713), a soldier, privateer, and later an officer on Long Island. Around 1695, Capt. Thomas Townsend gifted land in Massapequa named Fort Neck to his son-in-law Jones and his wife, Freelove (Townsend's daughter). Jones's control of nearly 6,000 acres on the south shore afforded him the power to dominate and control whaling and fishing activities in the region. (SBU.)

Robert Moses exerted his influence and authority as a state appointed officer in numerous concurrent capacities to develop and execute unprecedented public works and infrastructure programs in New York State. To achieve his vision of a state park with beach access to the Atlantic, he initiated and devised the Jones Beach State Park complex. Accomplishing his vision required engineering comprehensive dredging projects, acquiring land, razing existing structures, and constructing diverse roadways to connect the mainland to the barrier island. Despite resistance from local residents and politicians, which included several "Save our Beaches" campaigns in the late 1920s and early 1930s, planning proceeded. This c. 1933 postcard published by the Long Island State Park Commission presents a westward-looking aerial view of the park. Identifiable landmarks include Ocean Parkway running vertically down the center; the 231-foot, pencil-shaped water tower near the top; the East Bathhouse to the left or south; and Zach's Bay to the right or north. (HOF.)

Jones Beach State Park was the place to see and to be seen. One way to accomplish both activities at once was to rent a rolling beach chair or strandkorb. Invented by German basket maker Wilhelm Bartelmann (1845–1930) in 1883, the original design had a single seat to provide people afflicted with health and mobility challenges with access to beaches. Subsequent models had multiple seats and windows. The use of canopied wicker and cane chairs later expanded, as these popular beach rentals signified affluence on the boardwalks of Atlantic City, Coney Island, and Jones Beach State Park. This postcard captures three beachgoers in a rolling chair being pushed along the boardwalk near the West Central Mall Building. In December 1946, the Long Island State Park Commission decided to sell the chairs and accepted bids for 16 of them. An advertisement published in the December 27, 1946, edition of the *Brooklyn Daily Eagle* stated they were "used for boardwalk use and are in fair condition, wicker construction, three wheels with pneumatic tires. Chairs have tops and glass windows side and rear." (HOF.)

Robert Moses's concept for a "peoples park" was grand, yet his design aesthetic was understated, with attention given to classical architectural details, balance, and symmetry. In the c. 1933 postcard above, guests are seated under a uniform row of tables fitted with striped umbrellas at the Luncheon Terrace on the boardwalk. These umbrellas were removed and stored indoors in the off-season and would be mended prior to the following season if necessary. The postcard below shows visitors on a walkway near Zach's Bay. In the foreground, two cut metal signs with silhouetted figures signify the locations of the "Bath House" and "Bay Bathing." The 231-foot water tower in the background was inspired by Campanile di San Marco, the bell tower of St. Mark's Basilica in Venice, Italy. (Both, HOF.)

Jones Beach Marine Theatre opened in 1952 on the north side of Zach's Bay. Constructed under the supervision of Robert Moses, the open-air amphitheater had a stage situated on the other side of a moat to enhance performances. However, this design feature presented logistical challenges as it required ferrying performers to it. The theater's first musical director was bandleader Guy Lombardo (1902–1977). In 1991, more seating was added by eliminating the moat. (HOF.)

In stark contrast to the ocean surf, the half-mile beach at Zach's Bay provided bathing in quiet waters at Field 5. Likely named after Zachariah James (c. 1812–1898) of Seaford, the bay is on the north side of Ocean Parkway in the area of the original Hill High Beach. In the 1920s and 1930s, these waters were frequently the site of swimming competitions and regattas. (PC.)

Jones Beach State Park, part of the New York State Office of Parks, Recreation, and Historic Preservation, has a lasting memorial in remembrance and honor of coworkers and their family members who perished on September 11, 2001. Dedicated in August 2003, it is located on the walkway leading to the Central Mall, Field 4. The monument was designed by Dawn Wesche of Wesche Monuments and Bruce Meirowitz of Jones Beach State Park. On the granite plaque, artist Peggy Meehan created an image of a woman being carried away from the twin towers by two firefighters. The accompanying inscription reads, "In every wave, in every breeze, we remember you." Several beaches across Long Island have established permanent September 11th memorials. (Both, HOF.)

In Every Wave,
In Every Breeze,
We Remember You

Three

SUFFOLK COUNTY, CENTRAL BEACHES

Between the 1880s and 1950s, Lake Ronkonkoma was a vibrant beach resort community enjoyed by both affluent New York City residents and locals. Proprietors of inns, pavilions, and restaurants around the lake's perimeter promoted their businesses for their immediate proximity to calm swimming conditions, sailing and boating opportunities, and excellent fishing. Lake Ronkonkoma encompasses 243 acres with more than two miles of shoreline. Retreating glaciers formed the freshwater kettle lake. (HOF.)

RAYNOR'S BEACH
LAKE RONKONKOMA

Finest Sandy Bathing Beach—5 Pavilions—Baseball Park and
Playground
A Private Pavilion for Your Sunday School Outing

George C. Raynor & Sons
Telephones 26 and 108   Lake Ronkonkoma

Telephone: Ronkonkoma 46

DUFFIELD'S
**WEST PARK BEACH
AND RESTAURANT
LAKE RONKONKOMA**

———

CANOES, BOATS
SLIDES, RAFTS
LAUNCH

———

BATHING

———

BASEBALL AND TENNIS
OUTINGS BY APPOINTMENT ONLY.
BEACH PARTIES.

PAULA BROWNE
INCORPORATED

Realtors

LAKE RONKONKOMA

———

CAMP SITES

BUNGALOWS, HOMES

PAVILIONS

HOTELS

INVESTMENTS

TURNER'S CORNER PARK
LAKE RONKONKOMA
LONG ISLAND

Boating—Bathing—Picnicking—Amusements—The Ideal Place to
Spend a Day, a Week, a Month or the Season—A Perfect Beach—
An Ideal Park.

The *Brooklyn Daily Eagle* featured Lake Ronkonkoma as a beautiful resort destination on July 19, 1926. The article described the area's natural setting and immense appeal to locals and visitors: "Lying in a valley all its own and surrounded by pine-clad hills, the lake, skirted by a gently sloping beach of white sand, has a circumference of approximately three miles . . . it has no visible source of supply and no known outlet, yet its waters rival in purity the crystal of the mountain brook." A combination of factors led to the decline of visitors over time to Lake Ronkonkoma, including the opening of new state parks and issues of water quality. Today, the lake area supports a wide spectrum of recreational activities, including fishing, picnicking, birdwatching, and exercising. This page of advertisements from the 1931 edition of *Long Island: The Sunrise Home Land* provides a glimpse of the many beaches and businesses that thrived in Lake Ronkonkoma. (SBU.)

Keeping Cool at Lake Ronkonkoma, L. I.

The community of Lake Ronkonkoma evolved from agricultural roots to a tourist haven around the turn of the 20th century. George C. Raynor (1868–1950) is credited with founding the first beach pavilion (Raynor's Beach) at the lake. Parcels of land fronting the water were reimagined as beaches, including Turner's Corner Park, Henry Max Becker's Beach, Ronkonkoma Shores Beach, Beverly Beach, Cedar Grove Beach, Duffield's West Park Beach, Blue Beach Pavilion, and North Beach. Pictured below is Yerk's Bathing Pavilion and Beach, established on the west shore by resort owner John Joseph "Jack" Yerk (1881–1944). It was a favorite local venue known for its bathing beach, shady picnic areas, and ice skating in the winter. (Above, PC; below, HOF.)

IN THE SHADE, YERK'S BEACH
LAKE RONKONKOMA
LONG ISLAND, N.Y.

Shelter Island is uniquely situated between the north and south forks of Long Island. Surrounded by Shelter Island Sound, Gardiners Bay, and the Peconic River, Shelter Island has both private and public beaches, including Crescent Beach, Shell Beach, Hay Beach, and Wades Beach. This c. 1918 postcard was produced by Henry Otto Korten and features a montage of waterfront scenes across the island. (SBU.)

Crescent Beach or Louis' Beach (named after hotel proprietor Louis Behringer) has been credited as the site of the first ferry-type service from Shelter Island to the north fork. This c. 1920 postcard, titled "Ferry to Shelter Island, North Haven," depicts the south fork connection. When cars were able to travel to the island, activity markedly increased with visitors seeking peace and tranquility amongst Shelter Island's protected beaches and shores. (HOF.)

Beachfront areas have played a pivotal role in Shelter Island's history. Fishing provided the Manhasset Indians and later colonists with sustenance. Beaches were sites of commerce with the transport of commodities such as sugar and (illegal) rum. Hay derived from northern Hay Beach was pilfered by British troops during the American Revolution. This c. 1900 photograph shows two women on Shelter Island harvesting shellfish on a tidal flat. (SIHS.)

The Bathing Pavilion and White Hill.   Shelter Island Heights, N. Y.

The Victorian-style, grand Prospect House hotel had its own dock and an impressive two-story bathing pavilion for guests seeking to swim in calm waters, dine, socialize, and be entertained at the beach. White Hill is the backdrop and marks the highest point on the island. Today, the site is the location of the Shelter Island Heights Beach Club. (HOF.)

New York Yacht Club Station, Shelter Island, N. Y.

The establishment of clubhouses, pavilions, and inns drew locals and residents to the Shelter Island beach areas. Station No. 5 of the New York Yacht Club opened in 1892 at the northern hamlet of Dering Harbor, in close proximity to the Manhasset House. *Summer Resorts on Long Island*, published by the Long Island Railroad Company (c. 1908), exalted the virtues of Shelter Island and the hotel: "As a resort, Shelter Island offers all the beauties of nature, coupled with every modern convenience. It affords excellent bathing, sailing, and attractive natural scenery. Conspicuously situated on the Shelter Island shore is the great Manhasset House, one of the finest hotels on the coast." (Above, HOF; below, SBU.)

Manhanset House, Shelter Island N. Y

Four

SUFFOLK COUNTY, NORTH SHORE BEACHES

P2822   Cottages, Asharoken Beach, Northport, L. I.   Photo Underwood & Underwood, N. Y.

Savvy lawyer and real estate developer William B. Codling (1855–1924) envisioned and developed Asharoken Beach as a resort community. In 1906, he advertised his properties in *Country Life in America* with the slogan, "Asharoken Beach: Water Both Sides—Heaven Overhead." Asharoken, named after the Mattinecock sachem, is an isthmus spanning Northport to Eatons Neck and bordered by Northport Bay, Duck Island Harbor, and Long Island Sound. (HOF.)

LONG ISLAND
The Sunrise HomeLand

1929

Island-wide Survey of Communities

To promote the economic potential and health benefits of living by Long Island's shores, vast numbers of community guidebooks and surveys were produced and distributed in the tristate area. This 1929 edition of *Long Island: The Sunrise Home Land* was published by the Long Island Chamber of Commerce. The cover illustration depicts a couple perched on a high bluff, looking eastward over Long Island's horizon, "where health and happiness go hand and hand." The intended audience of this book was prospective suburban home buyers. Content included descriptive reviews of communities and advertisements for new developments, realtors, and mortgage companies. This specific issue has a passage vividly describing New York's easternmost county: "Surf flashing in the sunshine; cool breezes blowing over fragrant pine forest and sparkling lakes, bays, and inlets; fertile farms and prosperous communities; miles of smooth motor highways affording wonderful views of land and sea—that is Suffolk County." (SBU.)

Sound Beach at Baiting Hollow, L. I.

Made in Germany. F. H. Corwin, Jeweler, Importer & Publisher, Riverhead, L. I. 258.

Since 1926, the Boy Scouts of America has operated Baiting Hollow Scout Camp, which includes activities on Long Island Sound. The beachfront in Baiting Hollow was the site of a historic event in equal rights on Long Island. As documented in the *Patchogue Advance* in August and September 1937, the site was made available to Girl Scouts, which gave young girls their first organized camping opportunity in Suffolk County. (PC.)

Sound View, at Port Jefferson, N. Y.

In the early 1900s, Belle Terre Estates was promoted as an exclusive community in Port Jefferson, overlooking Long Island Sound, Port Jefferson Harbor, and Mount Sinai Bay. Amenities included the members-only Belle Terre Club, an 18-hole golf course, and two private beaches comprised of "clean sand or pure white pebbles." The Neoclassical pergolas at the end of Cliff Drive were removed in 1934 after a fire destroyed the club. (PC.)

1926

With shorelines encompassing Centerport Harbor, Northport Harbor, and Northport Bay, the hamlet of Centerport has drawn visitors and families to its beaches since the mid-1800s for its still-water bathing, yachting, boating, and fishing. In 1949, the Town of Huntington Board of Trustees purchased a 24-acre beach property to create a new recreation area for the community and to alleviate overcrowding at Crab Meadow Beach in Northport. William K. Vanderbilt II (1878-1944) was a previous owner of this land. The acquisition laid the foundation for establishing Centerport Beach on the east side of Centerport Harbor. On the western side of the harbor are Fleets Cove Beach and the north shore's largest privately owned beach, Huntington Beach Community Association, pictured below in July 1940. (Above, PC; below, HHS)

This real-photo postcard of Cold Spring Harbor shows beach bathers and the two-story casino built by William Gerard in 1888. "Up and down the harbor from the Casino the view is lovely," reported *The New York Times* in 1889. "Salt-water bathing without the bullets of the rude surf is to be had at the door." Today, the casino is a clubhouse for the Cold Spring Harbor Beach Club. (CSH.)

Community Beach, Cold Spring Harbor, Long Island, N. Y.

Efforts led by residents of Cold Spring Harbor and Lloyd Harbor were instrumental toward establishing a local bathing beach. The Eagle Dock Foundation was founded in 1948 to ensure residents a public beach and bathing facilities. Nearly 100 residents donated $22,000 to purchase an initial two acres of beachfront land, which was later expanded. (HHS.)

FLEET'S NECK LOOKING W. CUTCHOGUE, L.I.

IN TOKEN OF THE

FRIENDSHIP

WHICH EXISTS BETWEEN US

TWO

THIS FRIENDLY MESSAGE POST

CARD

IS SENT FROM ME TO YOU.

This c. 1908 oversized postcard has an endearing sentiment of friendship and features an affixed real-photo cinderella stamp or poster stamp of the private beach at Fleets Neck, looking west in Cutchogue. This type of stamp resembles a postal stamp but is differentiated by its larger size and lack of a postal value. Pequash Avenue Beach or Fleets Neck Beach is a community beach in the Cutchogue–New Suffolk Park District. The article "Long Island Bungalow Life: It is Lived to Perfection In and Near Southold," published in the *Brooklyn Daily Eagle* on July 12, 1908, described how in a relative short time the area transformed into a beach community: "Truly the years are bringing changes along the bay . . . changes that prove how strongly the tide is setting toward the simple life in the open and that bring the rare enjoyment and rest afforded by contact with the woods and water." (PC.)

The friendship between Albert Einstein and David Rothman is captured in this photograph taken during the summer of 1939 on the beach at Horseshoe Cove in Nassau Point, on the southern peninsula within the hamlet of Cutchogue. Einstein immigrated to the United States in 1933 and was on the faculty at the Institute for Advanced Study at Princeton University. In March 1938, Einstein visited Mattituck to negotiate a summer lease for a bungalow with beach access, which would provide him the opportunity to sail. He rented a home in Nassau Point and returned again in 1939. That summer, Einstein's daughter Margot made a purchase in Rothman's store, and the following day Einstein visited it, seeking a pair of sandals. The largest pair available was a size 11 women's style, which he bought and is seen wearing in this photograph. Einstein and Rothman's friendship developed over a wide range of activities, from impromptu violin duets to conversations on scientific topics. Although Einstein did not visit Long Island in subsequent years, his time spent here left an indelible impression. (SHS.)

ROCKY POINT, LONG ISLAND SOUND.   EAST MARION, L. I.

East Marion is located on the north fork between Greenport and Orient in the town of Southold. In 1913, the area was described in a Long Island Rail Road publication as a place of beauty where "many a summer pilgrimage ends in rest and relaxation." The boulder-strewn Southold Town Beach at Rocky Point is depicted on this postcard printed by the Albertype Company of Brooklyn. (PC.)

EATON'S NECK, HUNTINGTON, L. I.

Eatons Neck is bounded by Huntington Bay, Northport Bay, and Long Island Sound. Named after colonial leader Theophilus Eaton (c. 1590–1658), the rocky beach depicted on this postcard suggests the dangers of navigating the surrounding waters. Shipwrecks spurred the construction of Eatons Neck Light in 1798. Hobart Beach, a town of Huntington Beach, is named after jurist and politician John Sloss Hobart (1738–1805), who inherited Eatons Neck and sponsored the lighthouse legislation. (PC.)

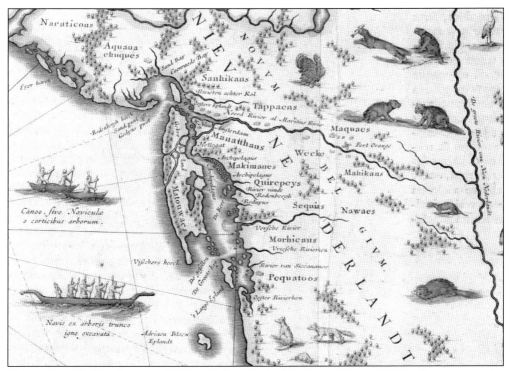

Fishers Island is 11 miles east of Orient Point within the town of Southold. The Pequot were the first inhabitants and called it Munnawtawkit. The name *Fishers* may have been inspired by Hoek van Visschers ("Fishers' Point") or Visschers hoeck, the name explorer Adriaen Block (c. 1567–c. 1627) gave Montauk Point in honor of cartographer Nicolaes Visscher (1618–1709). The area is noted on this c. 1640 map, titled *Nova Belgica et Anglia Nova*, by Willem Janszoon Blaeu (1571–1638). Brothers Edmond M. Ferguson and Walter Ferguson made significant financial investments to develop the island's infrastructure, including renovating the existing Lyles Beach Hotel in 1892. Renamed Munnatawket Hotel, reviews and advertisements touted its salt sea breezes, bathing, and "superior accommodations to seekers after rest, health, and pleasure." In 1926, the hotel was razed due to diminished use and structural problems. (Above, SBU; below, HOF.)

Booth House, Greenport, L. I.

This is a good place to go wading.
Marion

No. 684 Moore & Gibson Co. N. Y. Germany

In 1895, proprietor Charles Booth promoted beach bathing, fishing, and boating at Booth House on Sterling Creek in Greenport. The *Long-Islander* stated the inn prospered before the dawn of automobiles due to ferry access from New London and Shelter Island. Today, beaches in Greenport include Norman L. Klipp Park and Fifth Street Beach and Park. (PC.)

THE SIXTY-SEVEN STEPS, Greenport, L. I.

Located in Greenport is a nearly century-old, steep, wooden staircase that provides access to 67 Steps Beach. Storm-induced erosion has reduced the number of steps, though. In 2018, dedicated community members removed 1,100 pounds of beach litter and marine debris to improve the safety and preserve the area. The quantity and types of trash collected were logged and will provide valuable data for research studies. (SBU.)

6574 TERRACE OF CASINO CHATEAU DES BEAUX-ARTS
HUNTINGTON, L. I.

In 1906, brothers Andre, Jacques, and Louis Bustanoby, proprietors of Café des Beaux-Arts in New York City, commissioned the architectural firm Delano & Aldrich with Maurice Prevot to design a summer resort in Huntington. With unsurpassed amenities and expansive views of Huntington Bay and Long Island Sound, the 70-acre grounds provided beach bathing in calm waters and featured a hotel, casino/clubhouse, changing pavilions, and a pier for yachts. An article published on December 4, 1908, in the *Long-Islander* described a proposed neighboring community that did not come to fruition: "Beaux Arts Park is entrancing . . . The rolling hills, the undulating lawns, the bold cliffs and rugged headlands, the splendid beach, the sapphire sea water, the majestic sound, the passing night steamers, like fairy palaces of light, the white sails of yachts—the whole panorama from dawn to dawn is a constant kaleidoscope of color, grace, charm and splendor." This postcard shows the separate two-story casino building with its outdoor terraces overlooking the coast. Although both buildings are no longer standing, the history and legacy of Chateau des Beaux-Arts intrigues to this day. (PC.)

This photograph captures opening day of the private cabana colony at the Huntington Crescent Club Beach Casino on July 1, 1939. Located on the former site of Chateau des Beaux-Arts and directly on the shores of Huntington Bay, this area was later acquired by the Town of Huntington and today is the site of Crescent Beach. (HHS.)

The "Bathing Beach at Town Park, Huntington Harbor" was a popular summer resort area beginning in the late 1890s due in part to its accessibility by train and trolley. Pictured in the background is W. Raymond Selleck's Edgewater Hotel in Halesite. Open year-round, the hotel accommodated 100 guests and was promoted in the *Brooklyn Daily Eagle* for its boating, bathing, golf, and fishing opportunities. (SBU.)

ENTRANCE TO BEACH AREA

The c. 1937 postcard above and c. 1964 photograph below provide views of Sunken Meadow State Park, also known as Governor Alfred E. Smith State Park. Opened in 1927 and located in Kings Park on Long Island Sound, the terrain is variable, with high bluffs and a beach. Since 1926, the park has increased in size from the initial 200 acres purchased by the Long Island State Park Commission to more than 1,200 acres today. In addition to calm beach bathing, this popular park has many unique features, including golf courses designed by Alfred H. Tull (1897–1982), the northernmost two-mile stretch of the Long Island Greenbelt Trail, a bridle path, and a launch area for water activities such as windsurfing. (Both, HOF.)

71

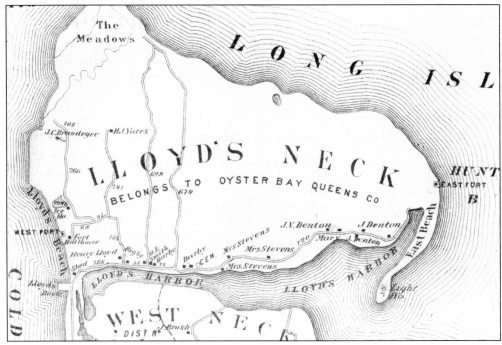

This map from *Atlas of Long Island* (F.W. Beers, 1873) shows Lloyd Neck belonging to the town of Oyster Bay, Queens County. Lloyd Beach is noted on the west (left) fronting Cold Spring Harbor, while East Beach (right) is surrounded by Lloyd Harbor and Huntington Bay. The land became part of the town of Huntington in 1885. In 1926, Lloyd Neck and West Neck merged to form the incorporated village of Lloyd Harbor. (SBU.)

Steamboats departing from New York City would bring travelers to Columbia Grove, the hotel opened in 1878 by George Van Ausdall Sr. (1838–1910). The resort complex in Lloyd Neck offered beach bathing in serene waters, boating, and carriage rides. Today, there are several beaches and parks with shorefront access in this vicinity, including Lloyd Neck Beach, West Neck Beach, Caumsett State Park, Target Rock National Wildlife Refuge, and East Beach. (HHS.)

This c. 1900 real-photo postcard by Arthur S. Greene (1867–1955) captures beachgoers in Long Island Sound relaxing on the sand and wading in waters at Miller Place. This location was enjoyed as a summer retreat by members of the Auxiliary Society of the Association of Working Girls Societies of New York. Between 1890 and 1909, the association purchased 18 acres with existing houses it renamed Holiday House and Harbor House. An article in the May 1894 issue of *Scribner's* stated: "Life at Holiday House in summer is a very free and happy condition. What have we of life without some familiarity with the country and its pleasures, some knowledge of nature itself! Though the new and strange features of country life—the woods, the cliffs, the beach—may have inspired something very much like fear in the first visitors at Holiday House, each successive sojourn only adds to the deep enjoyment of that first experience." (MPMSHS.)

Cedar Beach Main and Cedar Beach West are situated between Mount Sinai Harbor to the south and Long Island Sound to the north. Cedar Beach Main also marks the beginning of the 21-mile Benjamin Tallmadge Historical Trail to Mastic, which commemorates the historical significance of the location, named in honor of the Setauket-born military officer, politician, and George Washington's chief spy officer during the Revolutionary War. (MPMSHS.)

South of Cutchogue is the community of New Suffolk. It has calm bathing beaches fronting Peconic Bay, including New Suffolk Beach, a town of Southold beach. To the west is Kimogenor Point, which initially flourished as a summer bungalow colony in the early 1900s. The community was touted for its offerings of fine bathing, entertainment, and sailing. The homes later transitioned into year-round residences. (PC.)

SHORT BEACH, ST. JAMES, LONG ISLAND, N.Y.

Beaches have been documented in Smithtown records since the 17th century. In the village of Nissequogue, Short Beach (above) is located on the western part of the peninsula on Smithtown Bay and Long Island Sound, while Long Beach (below) and Otto Schubert Beach are situated to the east. Between Short Beach and Long Beach is the David Weld Sanctuary, a 125-acre preserve owned by The Nature Conservancy that includes 1,800 feet of rocky beachfront shaped by glaciers. Open to the public, the preserve provides opportunities to connect with nature through hiking, bird watching, and related activities. These postcards were produced around 1940. (Both, TSL.)

LONG BEACH, SMITHTOWN, LONG ISLAND, N.Y.

Early colonial settlers of Smithtown had rights to and ownership of thatch beds on the beaches. From these beds, hay and straw were derived to support agricultural activities. Protective measures, such as installing fences, were taken to ensure the integrity of the beds were maintained and to keep horses and cattle at bay. Later, as land became privately owned, several community members, including local developer and justice of the peace George S. Hodginkson (1860–1928), served on the town park and beach committee to expand access to the public. This c. 1900 photograph includes members of the Handley and Lawrence families. They are gathered at the Handleys' beachfront dock on the Nissequogue River enjoying a clambake, a festive and popular way for family and friends to socialize on the beach over food. Richard H. Handley (1848–1914) owned more than 250 acres in Smithtown, including waterfront access to the river and bay. (TSL.)

A 8071 At Crab Meadow Beach, Northport, L. J.

The land comprising Crab Meadow Beach in Northport is documented in 17th-century Town of Huntington records. However, ownership of the acreage was not clearly defined over time, and in the early 1900s, private cottages dotted the shore. In 1909, attorney Willard N. Baylis was retained by the town to assess historical records. He determined the balance of the land and title belonged to the town. By 1920, a town park was established. (HHS.)

CRAB MEADOW BEACH, NORTHPORT, LONG ISLAND, N. Y.

The original pavilion at Crab Meadow in Northport was operated by William B. Burt. The Town of Huntington later acquired land from him, and in 1938, a new pavilion opened. A Works Progress Administration (WPA) project, the building featured new amenities, including lockers, showers, and a sun deck. This postcard by the Tomlin Art Company shows a view of the Mediterranean-inspired structure designed by Huntington architect David Dusenberry (1883–1960). (HHS.)

Orient Point County Park, Orient Point Lighthouse, Orient Beach State Park, and Plum Island are among Long Island's most northern and eastern beach areas. The state park was announced on October 7, 1929, under the aegis of the Long Island State Park Commission. Encompassing land formerly named Long Beach, the area is known for its rocky terrain, maritime forest, and distinct wildlife, including endangered ospreys, eagles, and hawks. (PC.)

The Bay House   Bathing Beach   Orient, Long Island, N. Y.

The Bay House (left), located near the wharf in the hamlet of Orient, had a bathing beach facing Orient Harbor. According to an account in the *Corrector* published on May 29, 1897, several local residents bought the property for $2,000 to prevent its purchase by a proprietor with rumored intentions to sell liquor. (HOF.)

In this c. 1890 photograph, the Wells family is pictured on a horse-drawn buggy en route to the beach by Goldsmith's Inlet in Peconic, in the town of Southold. Beaches in the township include Kenney's Beach, McCabe's Beach, New Suffolk Beach, Norman E. Klipp Park or Gull Pond Beach, and Town Beach. (SHS.)

This rare real-photo postcard documents a bathing beach and swimmers along Port Jefferson Harbor. Port Jefferson has a rich maritime history. Its thriving shipbuilding industry commenced in 1797, spurring its name change from Drowned Meadow in 1896. The extension of the Long Island Rail Road in 1873 coupled with economic shifts were catalysts for reimagining the community as a tourist haven. (THSGPJ.)

West Bathing Beach, Port Jefferson, N. Y.

Port Jefferson has stretches of beaches on Long Island Sound (East Beach and West Beach) and within the bounds of Port Jefferson Harbor. The beaches have suffered erosion from severe storm events, including hurricanes. The village has been proactive in securing funding and executing restoration projects, including the construction of a new seawall. These two c. 1910 postcards illustrate early bathing beaches on the harbor. West Bathing Beach, near Beach Street (above), was a popular place for swimming and launching rowboats. Today, the former beach area is a passive play park. The bathing beach at the east side of the harbor (below) is situated among a backdrop of sandy bluffs. Kayaking and beachcombing are popular activities here today. (Above, PC; below, THSGPJ.)

Port Jefferson Bathing Beach   1910

North Shore Beach at Rocky Point was established as a bungalow colony in 1928. William Randolph Hearst's newspaper the *Daily Mirror* was the catalyst for development of the area. In an attempt to increase business, the company purchased nearly two miles of beachfront land and offered annual subscribers the exclusive opportunity to purchase lots for $89.50 each. By 1929, sales were brisk, and cottages were constructed on high bluffs with expansive views of Long Island Sound. The North Shore Beach Property Owners Association was also formed that year. Membership amenities included access to a private beach and a clubhouse. During this time, the Long Island Rail Road offered service between Port Jefferson and Wading River, which ensured ease of transportation to the area (it ceased in 1938). The year-round population was 100, but during the summer months it surged to 2,000, according to the *Long Island Gazetteer, A Guide to Historic Places* compiled by Arthur R. Macoskey in 1939. Over time, the vacation homes were winterized and transformed into year-round residences. (HOF.)

Photographer Arthur S. Greene (1867–1955) was born in Peterborough, England. He immigrated to the United States in 1889. Greene lived in Port Jefferson in 1894, where he managed a studio and later opened his own photography business. His work was documentary and focused on people and places on the north shore of Long Island, particularly in the town of Brookhaven. He produced hundreds of real-photo postcards over the course of his lifetime. This c. 1909 example is postmarked July 27, 1911, and captures a day at the beach in Shoreham, between Rocky Point and Wading River. To the left, three women are perched among the tall grasses and shrubbery high on the bluff. Bungalows, beachgoers, and Long Island Sound are visible in the background. The structure with the pointed roof at center was a beach pavilion. It had a large open area that functioned as a dance floor and observation deck. The lower area had bathhouses. Running parallel to the pavilion was a large, multilevel wooden stairway that provided access to the beach. (HOF.)

LIFE GUARD STATION, SOUND BEACH, LONG ISLAND, N. Y.

In 1929, the *Daily Mirror* newspaper brokered sales of lots in Sound Beach as it did for neighboring Rocky Point (see page 81). The Sound Beach Property Owners' Association was mindful of protecting the area's natural features while furthering the hamlet's development. The private Pickwick Beach and Scotts Beach are vulnerable to erosion from weather. Several shoreline stabilization projects have been completed in the past five years. (PC.)

The Brooklyn North District Epworth League Bathing Pavilion at So. Jamesport, L. I. With love – Clara.

The Brooklyn North District Epworth League maintained a Fresh Air Home and held institutes at South Jamesport beginning in the early 1900s. An aim of the Methodist association was to provide disadvantaged children from New York City with free summer camps. This c. 1900 postcard shows the bathing pavilion on the beach by the Peconic River. (HOF.)

Located in the hamlet of Southold is Founders Landing Park. This c. 1910 postcard shows the Wharf House at Founders Landing with a path leading to the beach on Southold Bay. In 1640, English Puritans began departing the New Haven Colony of Connecticut and landed at this site. Today, the beach area is part of the Southold Park District, which was established in 1907. (HOF.)

In this c. 1900 photograph, a group of family and friends are gathered for a picnic clambake in Southold amongst a rocky outcrop on Long Island Sound. Skirts, puff-sleeved blouses, and hats were standard attire. Women, men, and children would dress formally for these casual beach outings regardless of the temperature. Boulders and bluffs, distinguishable features of north shore beaches, can be seen in the background. (SHS.)

P.S. This photo was taken at West Meadow Beach near Stony Brook L.I. and simply shows a group of summer boarders none of whom I knew.

1.00

CORRESPONDENCE HERE

Jan 11, 1938 –
I was working for Mr. A. S. Greene, the photographer and was with him in the summer of 1907, when he took this photo. The tack holes were caused by my having tacked it on the wall of my room in Cascadilla Building at Ithaca while I'm Cornell. I occupied that room for three years. 1908 to 1911 –
A. G. Hallock.

This photograph and likely the real-photo postcard were produced in the summer of 1907 by prolific Long Island photographer Arthur S. Greene (1867–1955). The note on the card was written in 1938 by A.G. Hallock. Reflecting on his past, Hallock states he worked for Greene and accompanied him when this photograph was taken. In his "p.s.," Hallock identified the location as West Meadow Beach, near Stony Brook, and the subjects as summer boarders. The first public suggestion of a park at West Meadow Beach was made by local resident and philanthropist Eversley Childs (1867–1953) to the Town of Brookhaven board on May 19, 1908. Later that year on November 21, Childs and others conveyed their "land at West Meadow for the uses and purposes of a public park forever." (Both, TVHS.)

The subjects of these two real-photo postcards, produced a year apart, are summer boarders of all ages at Pine View House, the c. 1710 Eleazer Hawkins Homestead in Stony Brook. The c. 1907 photograph above is attributed to Israel Hawkins, and the c. 1906 photograph below was taken by Arthur S. Greene. The location is the vicinity of Sand Street Beach, Shipman's Beach, and West Meadow Beach in Stony Brook. Evelina Hawkins and her proprietor husband, Israel G. Hawkins, opened the boardinghouse and hotel in 1898; it accommodated up to 25 guests. It was situated near a pine grove within a five-minute walk to the beaches. (Both, TVHS.)

Shipman's Beach from the Bluff   Stony Brook, Long Island, N. Y.

Shipman's Beach (above) and Stony Brook Beach or Sand Street Beach (below) overlook Stony Brook Harbor. Popular activities here include swimming, kayaking, and fishing. Wetlands and tidal salt marshes provide habitat to shorebirds including egrets, osprey, and piping plovers. To the east, the area adjoins West Meadow Beach along Long Island Sound and Smithtown Bay. Sources suggest the sand spit formations along this shoreline are 6,000 years old. In the 1920s, a summer bungalow community with nearly 100 cottages was established. All but four buildings and the Victorian-style Gamecock Cottage (c. 1876) were removed in 2004 to foster restoration of the peninsula's ecosystem. (Both, PC.)

Bathing Beach, Stony Brook, N. Y.

BATHING BEACH, WILDWOOD STATE PARK, LONG ISLAND, N.Y.

In 1925, the Long Island State Park Commission announced the establishment of Wildwood State Park in Wading River. The original 600 acres were acquired through gift and by purchase of land formerly owned by millionaire Roland Greene Mitchell (1841–1906). Greene's estate in Great Neck was named Wildwood. Early descriptions of the park promoted campgrounds with platform tent sites, a bathing beach on Long Island Sound, and beautiful woodlands. The 1933 guidebook *New York State Parks* singled out Wildwood for having one of "the few remaining stands of virgin timber on Long Island." In 2018, new modern prototype vacation rental cottages, the first of their type on Long Island, were opened at the park. (Above, MMSCL; below, TSL.)

Five

SUFFOLK COUNTY, SOUTH SHORE BEACHES

Today, Ocean Avenue in Amagansett is named Indian Wells Highway and leads to the namesake beach. In his poem "Afternoon: Amagansett Beach," longtime East Hampton summer resident and poet John Hall Wheelock (1886–1978) described the scenery he observed throughout his lifetime: "Great dunes with their pale grass, and on the beach / Driftwood, tangle of bones, an occasional shell / Now coarse, now carven and delicate / To lost time, old oceanic secrets." (EHHS.)

Devon Colony was founded in 1908 on 600 hilly acres in Amagansett by Cincinnati-based executives of Proctor & Gamble under the entity Gardiner's Bay Company. The Gardiner's Bay Boat Club fronting Gardiner's Bay was incorporated in 1911. The club was reestablished as the Devon Yacht Club on November 8, 1916. Access to a sandy beach, communal clubhouse, and a dock were among the original amenities of the club. (EHHS.)

A Long Island Rail Road publication described Amagansett in 1913 as "immediately upon the ocean and is surrounded by a rich farming region, with an assured great future." The hamlet is home to several town of East Hampton beaches. Examples of bayfront beaches are Barnes Hole, Big Albert's Landing, and Lazy Point. Ocean beaches with surf bathing include Atlantic Avenue and Indian Wells. (PC.)

In April 1936, *The New York Times* announced that Richard B. Allen's (1875–1954) corporation purchased 234 acres between Amagansett and Napeague. It was here that Allen developed the private oceanfront colony named Beach Hampton. By July 1926, the construction of 50 cottages was near completion. The layout formed a distinct enclave, as illustrated on this map by Harry A. Chandler. Advertisements stated the residences were "air conditioned by nature" and priced starting at $2,900 for a house and $300 for a lot. Amenities included a residents-only sandy beach and a surf club. The elevated perspective of this map drew attention to transportation options with notations for the Montauk Highway, the Long Island Rail Road, and the New London Ferry. In addition to surf activities, Gardiner's Bay and Devon Yacht Club are also shown to the north. Residences in Beach Hampton were occupied by 1938; however, on September 21 of that same year, the devastating and deadly Great New England Hurricane hit Long Island and destroyed most of the buildings in the community. (EHL.)

A CLUB FOR THE FAMILY
A Kiddies Paradise
AMITY BEACH & YACHT CLUB
on MERRICK ROAD just beyond AMITYVILLE

ACTUAL PHOTOGRAPH OF CLUBHOUSE ON GREAT SOUTH BAY

BUNGALOWS ABSOLUTELY THE BEST BUY ON LONG ISLAND
3, 4 or 5 rooms and complete bath and porch

HOMES BUILT TO ORDER AND SOLD ON RENTAL BASIS

Our own PRIVATE SANDY BATHING BEACH 1¾ miles from Jones Beach
—Tie your boat in your own yard—Tennis and Handball courts—canoes,
rowboats—dancing, dining—children's playground with all equipment that
kiddies love—miniature golf course—wonderful fishing and crabbing—duck
shooting—Gas, electricity—Concrete streets and sidewalks—Nothing left
out.

Developed by

GEORGE J. BROWN
225 WEST 34th STREET LOngacre 5-4905 NEW YORK CITY

This c. 1931 advertisement announced the opportunity to purchase a home in Amityville, located south of Merrick Road on the Great South Bay. The site was less than two miles from Jones Beach and included access to a private beach. In the early 1930s, George J. Brown's firm built several bungalow properties on undeveloped farmland adjacent to the associated Amity Beach and Yacht Club. (SBU.)

According to historian Paul Bailey, African Americans visited Hemlock Beach, south of mainland Amityville, every August from 1841 to 1910 to celebrate the emancipation of slavery in New York. In the early 1900s, the weeklong event was held at Van Nostrand's pavilion and hotel. Severe storms in 1914 caused irreparable damage to the area. In October 1915, the *Brooklyn Daily Eagle* declared the "passing of Hemlock Beach as a summer resort." (PC.)

The Pavilion, Hemlock Beach, Amityville, L. I.

SWIMMING POOL, BAY SHORE BEACH, BAY SHORE, L. I., N. Y.

In March 1924, Bay Shore Beach Inc. announced construction of 600 modern and fireproof bathhouses, a large swimming pool, and a pavilion on the site of the original Benjamin Bathing Beach, which was destroyed by fire in November 1923. When the new complex opened on the bay in the summer of 1924, the company proclaimed it offered the "finest and safest bathing beach on Long Island." (PC.)

KIDDIE MERRY-GO-ROUND, BABYLON BEACH, BABYLON, L. I., N. Y.

Developer Cadman H. Frederick (c. 1881–1961) commented on Babylon Beach in October 1927: "This bathing beach . . . built on my property, has over 1,000 bathhouses and the largest outdoor tiled swimming pool in America. Over 50,000 people bathed at this Babylon bathing beach this summer, in spite of the fact that eleven out of fourteen weekends were rainy." Town of Babylon ocean beaches include Cedar, Gilgo, and Overlook. (SBU.)

The Bathing Dock, Blue Point, L. I.

Five Mile Look Bathing Beach on Great South Bay, at the foot of Blue Point Avenue in Blue Point, was a favorite summer destination, as evidenced by these postcards from July 1916. *Long Island Gazetteer: A Guide to Historic Places* (1939) described the charms of Blue Point: "The extensive shorefront, fine bathing beach, and recreation pier, and above all, the ocean breezes and unparalleled climate, render the resort most attractive and healthful." The dock at the beach was a site for ferry departures to and from Water Island and Cherry Grove on Fire Island. (Both, BBPPL.)

The history of Bridgehampton is inextricably connected with the sea. Access to beaches afforded its early settlers with subsistence. The extension of the Long Island Rail Road to the hamlet in 1870 spurred the founding of a summer colony and consequently new economic opportunities. The Twyeffort family's summer home in Bridgehampton was named Rusticana. They are pictured here with friends seated under an arbor on the beach. (TBM.)

Cap Tree Island, N. Y.

Captree Island is between the mainland and the eastern end of Jones Beach Island, north of the 340-acre Captree State Park. Automobile access to Captree Island was made possible in 1951 with the construction of Great South Bay Bridge. Prior to the completion of the Fire Island Inlet Bridge, travel to Fire Island was by private boat or ferry from Captree Island. (SBU.)

The *East Hampton Star* proclaimed in 1928, "The history of the bathing beach is practically the history of East Hampton as a summer resort." The foot of Ocean Avenue in the village of East Hampton is depicted on this c. 1911 postcard. Horse-drawn buggies, automobiles, and bicycles are parked on the sandy road. Two women are pictured walking south toward Main Beach and a popular pavilion owned by Andrew Culver. (EHL.)

Founded in 1891, the private Maidstone Club in East Hampton has its own beach, pool, golf course, individual cabanas, and clubhouse. According to a 1927 article in the *East Hampton Star*, "A committee was appointed to consider improvements upon the bathing beach at the club; and the next year swimming pool and cabanas were started." This postcard shows the additions completed just one year later and available to members in July 1928. (HOF.)

Born and raised in East Hampton, Aronio "Roney" Marasca (1915–1981) is pictured on the beach in East Hampton. He worked as a haul seiner and a lifeguard, served in the US Coast Guard and US Navy during World War II, and was proprietor of the Chowder Bowl eatery at the Main Beach Pavilion in the village of East Hampton. (EHL.)

This postcard, published by E.J. Edwards of the Albertype Company in Brooklyn, captures the launch of a whale boat by its crew on a beach in East Hampton. Beginning in the 17th century, Native Americans' engagement in and control of whaling activities in the east end (south shore) waters shifted to the behest of English settlers. Sperm oil and whale oil derived from blubber were profitable commodities. (HOF.)

E.J. EDWARDS,   WHALING BOAT AND CREW, EAST HAMPTON, L.I.

This undated photograph, titled "Fishing at the Beach, East Hampton, New York," documents the practice of haul seine fishing. Ralph Henry Gabriel described the process in *The Evolution of Long Island* (1921): "The most important possession . . . was a huge seine (net), sometimes fully three-quarters of a mile in length. A small, weathered, board shack on the beach was called 'headquarters' . . . When the surface of the bay was rippled . . . swiftly fish would be surrounded. Each boat would drop overboard the segment of the net it carried. The pieces would be coupled together and the ends of the great seine brought to the shore as near as possible to the headquarters shack. Horses would be hitched to the net at the water's edge and the fish drawn slowly up the beach. When all was done, a heap of glistening 'bunkers,' perhaps a hundred thousand or more, would lie piled up on the sand." (EHL.)

Long Island's beaches have inspired artists for several centuries. In 1877, a group of highly esteemed artists, writers, and architects formed the Tile Club. At weekly gatherings in New York City, members conversed about artistic endeavors while painting ceramic tiles and working in new mediums in response to the period's aesthetic shift from landscape painting to decorative arts. Associates included Augustus Saint-Gaudens, Winslow Homer, William Merritt Chase, and Stanford White. Taking excursions by boat, train, and stagecoach, they explored Long Island. This c. 1878 hand-painted tile was created by founding Tile Club member Arthur Quartley (1839–1886). In delicate shades of blue, the tile depicts a girl seated on the sand in East Hampton gazing at the sea. Painters, sculptors, and photographers moved from New York City to the east end in the mid-20th century to establish residences and studios, particularly between Bridgehampton and Montauk. The communities afforded privacy, cultivated camaraderie, and spurred creativity for many revered and influential artists. (EHL).

The Sea Spray on the Dunes

Easthampton,
Long Island, N. Y.

Set among the dunes was the Sea Spray Inn at Main Beach in the village of East Hampton. Formerly the home of Josiah Mulford, the building was located on Main Street and used as a hotel. In 1902, it was relocated to the oceanfront and expanded. The inn was one of the most popular east end locales until the main house was consumed by fire in February 1978. The cottages remained intact. The land was later acquired by the Town of East Hampton. The aerial photograph below of Main Beach dates from between 1930 and 1950. With Ocean Avenue running down the middle as a reference point, pictured at lower left is the bathing pavilion, and at lower right is the inn with cottages. (Both, EHL.)

A Colorful Scene on the Great South Bay Bathing Beach at Heckscher State Park
East Islip near Lindenhurst Long Island, N. Y.

Located at the Great South Bay in East Islip is Heckscher State Park. Named after philanthropist August Heckscher (1848–1941), the park opened in 1929 after six years of lawsuits between local landowners and the Long Island State Park Commission. With support from Gov. Alfred E. Smith, the Robert Moses–led project proceeded. Today, the park is comprised of 1,600 acres with a beach, nature trails, and shaded picnic areas. (PC.)

Greetings from **East Moriches Long Island**

This c. 1930 linen textured postcard by Tichnor Brothers of Boston features an array of images representing water activities in East Moriches, which is located between Center Moriches and Eastport, with Moriches Bay to the south. In 1944, the Long Island Association extolled the area for its recreational coastal activities: "In the Moriches all forms of water sports, bathing, boating, sailing and fishing are enjoyed under ideal conditions." (TSL.)

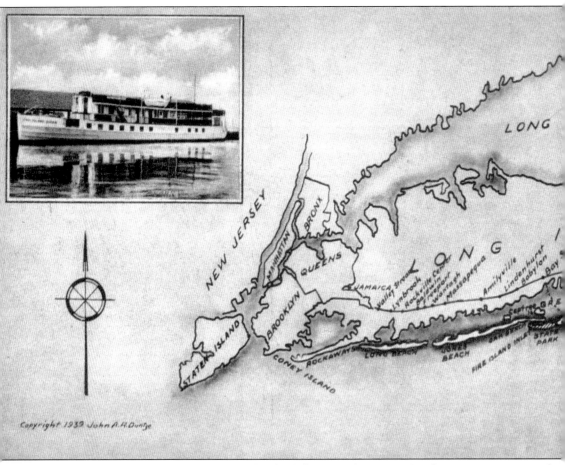

Copyright 1939 John A.H. Dunje

Fire Island is a 32-mile barrier beach island fronting the Great South Bay, interconnected bays, and the Atlantic Ocean. Much of the island's natural state is preserved due to grassroot efforts of dedicated residents, concerned citizens, and state and national legislative initiatives. Seventeen distinct and diverse beachfront communities comprise the 26-mile stretch within the Fire Island National Seashore (FINS): Atlantique, Cherry Grove, Corneille Estates, Davis

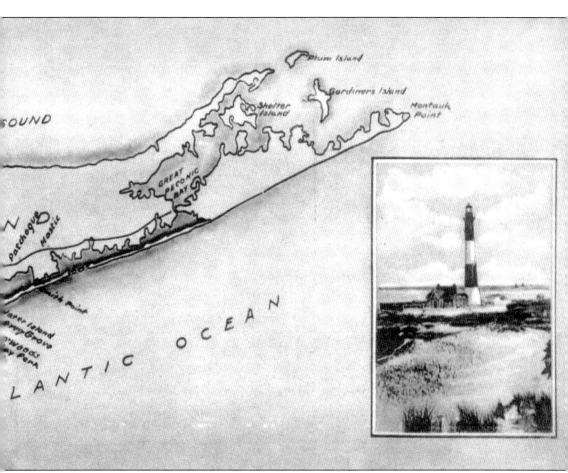

Park, Dunewood, Fair Harbor, Fire Island Pines, Kismet, Lonelyville, Ocean Bay Park, Ocean Beach, Point O'Woods, Robbins Rest, Saltaire, Seaview, Summer Club, and Water Island. Rare ecological habitats are found throughout the FINS, including at Sunken Forest and the Otis Pike Fire Island High Dune Wilderness. This c. 1939 oversized postcard highlighting Fire Island was illustrated by Ocean Beach resident and artist John Duntze. (PC.)

Charles Henry Miller (1842–1922) received public recognition for his artistry and has works represented in museum collections. His portfolio of illustrations titled *New York and Long Island Landscapes* (1889) documents serene scenery across the island. This c. 1882 engraving captures the historic Fire Island Lighthouse on its natural sandy terrain, east of present-day Robert Moses State Park and part of the Fire Island National Seashore. (SBU.)

This postcard provides an aerial view of the Fire Island Light Station located between the bay and ocean. Construction of the 168-foot stone tower was completed in 1858, replacing the original 1826 structure. It remains an important navigational aid and is an educational site due to the efforts of the Fire Island Lighthouse Preservation Society in cooperation with the National Park Service. (PC.)

Robert Cushman Murphy (1887–1973) was an ornithologist, naturalist, and Lamont curator of birds at the American Museum of Natural History. His research and writings, such as *August on Fire Island Beach* (1933), influenced the establishment of Fire Island National Seashore in 1964 and Rachel Carson's seminal book *Silent Spring* (1962). Among his publications are 600 scientific articles and *Fish-Shape Paumanok: Nature and Man on Long Island* (1964). (SBU.)

On June 14, 1964, a total of 700 guests, including planner Robert Moses, attended the dedication ceremony to open the Fire Island Inlet Bridge, which linked Fire Island to Jones Beach Island, and the naming of Robert Moses State Park in his honor. Formerly Fire Island State Park, the nearly five-mile stretch of shoreline is located at the western end of the island (pictured to the left or south). (HOF.)

Surf Hotel, Fire Islan

Proprietor David Sturgis Sprague Sammis (1818–1895) purchased 120 acres of land in 1855 on Fire Island east of the lighthouse in present-day Kismet. This advertisement for his Surf Hotel appeared in *Illustrated Long Island* (1883). Promoted as "The only natural sea-shore resort in America, long famous for its invigorating breezes, healthfulness and quiet enjoyment," the beach property was expanded by Sammis several times to accommodate 500 guests at a cost of more than $200,000. A half-mile-long, 20-foot-wide plank walk was installed so guests could access the shoreline without walking on the hot sand. Decades later business declined, and in 1892, Sammis sold the property to the State of New York for $210,000. The state's intention was to quarantine immigrants here, specifically passengers arriving in New York who were afflicted with cholera. In 1908, this acreage formed part of Fire Island State Park, the first state park on Long Island. It later became part of the Fire Island National Seashore. The building was destroyed by fire in 1918. (SBU.)

Black cherry trees growing behind dunes inspired the name Cherry Grove on Fire Island. Beginning in the 1920s, New York's LGBTQ community found safe havens in Cherry Grove and Fire Island Pines. The hamlets are nationally recognized for their historic contributions to civil rights. (TSL.)

In 1947, the Home Guardian Company of New York began advertising for a new beach cottage community named Fire Island Pines. The site was Lone Hill, the former location of a Coast Guard station. With lots starting at $275, the Pines was touted for its "velvet-like" white sand beach. This full-page advertisement appeared in the June 29, 1952, issue of the *Patchogue Advance*. (NYSHN.)

ONE AND ONE-HALF MILES OF OCEAN PLAYGROUND

with Protected Yacht Harbor...

BUY NOW!

ON THE ATLANTIC OCEAN
AND
GREAT SOUTH BAY
OPPOSITE
Sayville, Long Island

Direct Ferry Service
1:15 P. M. DAILY

FIRE ISLAND PINES

LOTS $275 AND UP

MINIMUM 3 LOTS

— EASY TERMS —

Important? All Lot Reservations Made at Office Subject to Your Inspection and Approval at the Property.

Buy Now For The Future . . . Don't Delay!

HOME GUARDIAN COMPANY OF NEW YORK

Surf View Walk, Ocean Beach, Fire Island, N. Y.

Ocean Beach on Fire Island is bounded to the west by Surf View Walk, pictured in this c. 1920s postcard published by the local variety store Busch's Corner. The community was described on postcards: "Seven miles from the mainland is the Village of Ocean Beach, the most picturesque summer resort on the Atlantic Coast." (TSL.)

From the 1910s to 1940s, Bellport Village and Brookhaven Hamlet residents sailed on the *Mildred A.* and *Ruth* to Taffy Point on Fire Island, later the site of the Old Inlet Club. The inlet naturally closed in 1825. In 2012, a breach during Hurricane Sandy created a gap and caused the inlet to reopen. Today, it is part of the Otis Pike High Dune Wilderness Area. (PC.)

In 1894, residential dwellings on Fire Island were founded at Point O'Woods. The Long Island Chapter of the Chautauqua Association, a spiritual and adult education congregation, established a meetinghouse to accommodate 2,000 guests. Within four years, the chapter declared bankruptcy. Former members established the Point O'Woods Association and acquired the land between Ocean Bay Park and Oakleyville. Pictured is a 1915 advertisement for the former inn. (SBU.)

The INN and BATHING BEACH
POINT O' WOODS, L. I.

Ocean on one side   *Bay on the other*

Point O' Woods is a summer colony of the highest class. Practically six miles out in the open sea.   *For rates and information apply to*

POINT O' WOODS ASS'N
C. W. NASH, *Sup't*

BAYSHORE,   AFTER JUNE 1ST
    L. I.   POINT O' WOODS, L. I.

Social reformer and journalist Margaret Fuller (1810–1850) and her family tragically drowned near Point O'Woods when the barque *Elizabeth* hit a sandbar and sank. Author Henry David Thoreau (1817–1862) traveled to the island at the request of Fuller's friend and mentor Ralph Waldo Emerson (1803–1882) to aid in the search, but to no avail. (PC.)

SALTAIRE, Fire Island Beach.—Ocean Front

The village of Saltaire, between Kismet and Fair Harbor, was incorporated in 1917. It was the first community to obtain this status on Fire Island. The Fire Island Development Corporation acquired land in 1910 and launched an extensive marketing campaign for the summer homes it was building on the sand dunes. The starting price for a bungalow and plot was $1,500. Access from New York City was typically one hour via the Long Island Rail Road to Bay Shore followed by a 30-minute steamer ride. Early advertisements made appeals to family-oriented buyers, describing Saltaire as "a children's paradise" with pristine beaches touted as nature's playground. (Above, HOF; below TSL.)

SALTAIRE, Fire Island Beach.—Atlantic Walk

Ocean Scene at Water Island.

Between Davis Park to the east and Fire Island Pines to the west is the hamlet of Water Island on Fire Island. At the turn of the 20th century, hospitality businesses flourished, and the area emerged as a favorite vacation spot. By the 1930s, it was evolving into a very private community and today has limited ferry service from Sayville. (PC.)

This real-photo postcard by Merritt & Chapman Derrick & Wrecking Company captures the Norwegian steamship SS *Bodo* ashore on a sandbar at Gilgo Inlet. The steamer was stuck for eight days in March 1906 and freed by several tug boats without sustaining damage. The cargo contained bananas, which were thrown off the boat to lighten the load and subsequently enjoyed by residents of Amityville and surrounding communities. (HOF.)

The Bathing Beach, Good Grounds, L. I.

Formerly named Good Ground, Hampton Bays has several beaches within the hamlet, including Ponquogue Beach fronting the Atlantic and Meschutt Beach County Park on Great Peconic Bay. *This is Long Island* (1944), published by the Long Island Association, noted, "Pon Quogue Bridge gives access to surf bathing and surf fishing and opens to the public a long stretch of beautiful ocean beach unspoiled by crowds." (PC.)

Bayberry Point in the hamlet of Islip was developed as an experimental community by American industrialist Henry O. Havemeyer (1847–1907) and furthered by his son Horace. This c. 1924 postcard provides a vantage looking down a sandy, man-made waterway flanked by Moorish houses designed by architect Grosvenor Atterbury (1869–1956). The residences overlook the Great South Bay and were marketed for their accessibility to Fire Island beaches. (HOF.)

Mastic Beach is a peninsula surrounded by Bellport Bay, Narrow Bay, Moriches Bay, and the Forge River. In 1926, newspapers actively covered the rapid growth of this beach community. The *Brooklyn Citizen* was the developer and brokered sales of lots by subscription. An advertisement in the *Brooklyn Daily Eagle* stated subscribers could purchase lots on the Great South Bay for $89 each, which included access to a glistening white beach, boating, and fishing. More than 6,000 lots were sold within a three-month period. The development was constructed in phases. A beach scene and pavilion in section five are pictured on the postcard below. (Above, HOF; below, MMSCL.)

BEACH SCENE AND PAVILION, SECTION 5, MASTIC BEACH, LONG ISLAND, N. Y.

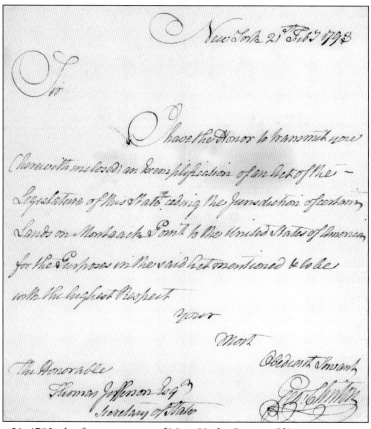

On February 21, 1793, the first governor of New York, George Clinton, wrote to Secretary of State Thomas Jefferson ceding land in Montauk to the United States. The Second United States Congress under George Washington subsequently appropriated $20,000 in March 1793 to build a lighthouse to aid navigation. Construction of the Montauk Point Light on Turtle Hill was completed in November 1796. Erosion has significantly reduced the historic structure's distance from the bluff to just 100 feet. In 2018, a $24 million shore stabilization project was announced to remediate this issue. The Montauk Historical Society stewards and owns the lighthouse complex, which is surrounded by Montauk Point State Park. Surf fishing, beachcombing, and hiking are popular activities at the park. (Above, SBU; below HOF.)

This 1926 advertisement published in *Long Island: The Sunrise Home Land* proclaimed, "Montauk Beach will be the Miami Beach of Long Island." Real estate magnate Carl G. Fisher's (1874–1939) bold vision to replicate his success in Miami Beach was realized by transforming Montauk from a pasture to a residential community and resort destination. Among his projects were developing the luxury hotel Montauk Manor, roadways, a railroad station, and a marina. (SBU.)

Opened in June 1927, Montauk Manor was a 200-room, Tudor Revival–style hotel commissioned by Carl G. Fisher. Designed by the firm Schultze & Weaver, the resort offered unparalleled views of shorelines, beach access, fishing, golf, tennis, yachting, and polo. Just a few years later, Fisher was bankrupt, and the hotel closed. The building was listed in the National Register of Historic Places in 1984. Today, it is a condominium complex. (HOF.)

Aero View, Montauk Manor   Montauk, Long Island, N. Y.

Ditch Plains Beach in Montauk is famed for surfing due to the coastline's unique geography. In the mid–18th century, dangerous conditions necessitated founding a US lifesaving station. In 1883, a total of 32 stations operated on Long Island, including Ditch Plains. (HOF.)

Walking or shifting dunes, woodlands, and a lake encompass Hither Hills State Park in Montauk. Part of Robert Moses's plan of expanding the New York state park system, it was founded in August 1924. With frontage on the Atlantic Ocean, Napeague Harbor, and Napeague Bay, Hither Hills provides the only oceanfront camping in New York state, as pictured on this real-photo postcard. (EHL.)

In 1915, a summer bungalow colony was established among the bluffs in North Sea, in the town of Southampton, on land owned by George R. Howell. In 1923, J. Hervey Topping, Arthur M. Havens, and Anthony Wilde purchased and expanded the North Sea Bathing Beach pavilion, which included 400 feet on Peconic Bay. The North Sea Beach Colony Association was later founded in 1947. (PC.)

On the eastern end of Jones Beach Island, in the town of Babylon, is the community of Oak Beach. This postcard, titled "Arrival of the Ice Boat," by E.C. Reiss shows two men pushing a cart loaded with a block of ice down a dock toward shore. (SBU.)

Patchogue was a prosperous and progressive village beginning in the early 1900s. The c. 1900 (above) and c. 1940 (below) postcards show the Smithport Bathing Beach on Patchogue Bay, technically a lagoon and part of the Great South Bay. Today, it is the site of the Patchogue Pool and Beach Club. *Souvenir of Patchogue, Long Island, New York* (1906) described the area here as "one of the finest inland bodies of water in the world . . . a strip of sand separates it from the ocean, and while the breakers roll high on the beach, hundreds of yachts are comfortably sailing on the quiet waters of the bay . . . the magnificent sweep of ocean beach affords an invigorating and inspiring sight." (Both, PML.)

The use of stagecoaches to travel from Brooklyn to the east end of Long Island had its beginnings prior to the American Revolution. The village of Quogue, in the town of Southampton, has drawn vacationers to its beaches since the 1830s. With the expansion of the Long Island Rail Road in the 1870s, the area transformed from a rural community to a vacation destination for affluent New Yorkers. (SBU.)

Wreck of the Naham Chapin on the Beach at Quogue, L. J.

"Wreck of the *Naham* [sic] *Chapin* on the beach at Quogue, L. J." [sic]" was published by M.L. Payne in January 1899. In 1897, an intense storm caused the *Nahum Chapin*, a three-masted schooner carrying coal, to break apart, and the crew could not be saved. The Quogue Life Station crew is pictured in front of the wreck. The anchor was recently refurbished and placed in front of the Quogue Library. (SBU.)

SAG HARBOR, L. I. THE HAVENS HOME AND BATHING BEACH.　　　Davis Dept. Store, Sag Harbor, L. I.

This c. 1906 postcard depicts Havens Home and the bathing beach in Sag Harbor overlooking Sag Harbor Bay. The large house in the background, today named Cormaria, was a summer residence built by Frank Colton Havens (1848–1917), a San Francisco real estate developer and descendant of a local founding family. (PC.)

The c. 1848 Italianate-style Cedar Island Light is located in Cedar Point County Park, Sag Harbor. Originally situated on an island, the Great New England Hurricane of 1938 formed a ridge of sand connecting it to the mainland. The lighthouse was decommissioned in 1934 and fell into disrepair. The Long Island Chapter of the United States Lighthouse Society is leading restoration efforts. (SBU.)

Sayville was home to many shorefront restaurants and dozens of boardinghouses and inns, particularly from the 1910s to 1940s. Notable beach areas on the Great South Bay included the pictured Cedarshore Hotel (Casino) and Beach at Handsome Avenue, Syke's Bathing Beach at Foster Avenue East, and Tidewater Inn (Shoreham Hotel). Sayville remains a site of ferry departures that provide access to several Fire Island beach communities. (PC.)

This c. 1950 photograph was taken in Shirley. The hamlet includes Shirley Beach, located on Bellport Bay and the Great South Bay. Smith Point County Park, one of Long Island's most popular ocean beaches for surfing and camping, is located on Fire Island. The park is named after early settler William "Tangier" Smith (1655–1705), who owned 64,000 acres on Long Island and 50 miles along the Atlantic Ocean. (MMSCL.)

DEED FROM WYANDANCH SACHEM TO LION GARDINER
FOR WEST BEACH, SOUTHAMPTON.

Be it knowne unto all men by this present writing, that this indenture covenant or agreement was made this **tenth** of **June** in the year of our Lord one thousand six hundred fifty and eight, betweene Wiandance Sachem of Paumanack, with his son Weeaycombon, and their associates, that is Sasagaktacow, Checanoe and Mawweehew, on the other side Lion Gardiner for himself his heires executors and assigns. That is to say that the afore-said Sachem Wiandance hath sold for a considerable somme of money and goods a certaine tract of beach lands with all the rest of the (word gone) that joynes to it and not sep-arated from it by water, which beach begins eastwards at the west end of Southampton bounds, and westward where it is separated by the water of the sea coming in out of the ocean sea, being bounded southward with the great sea, northward with the inland water. This land and the grasse there of for a range or run for to feed horses or cattell on. I say I have sould too the aforesayd Lion Gardener, his heires executors and assigns for ever, for the somme aforesayd, and a yearly rent of twenty five shillings a yeare, which yearley rent is to be payed to the aforesayd Sachem, his heires executors and assigns for ever in the eighth month called October, then to be demanded. But the whales that shall be cast upon this beach shall belong to me and the rest of the indians in their bounds, as they have beene anciently granted to them formerly by our fathers, and also liberty to cut in the summer time flags, bull rushes and such things as they make theire matts of, provided that they do no hurt to the horses that is thereon, and that this writing is to be understood, according to the letter, without any reservation or farther interpretation on it. We have both of us interchangeably set to our hands and seales.

This broadside represents part of a 1658 land deed for West Beach, Southampton. The parties were Wyandanch, sachem of the Montakettes (1615–1658); his son and his associates; and English-born Long Island settler Lion Gardiner (1599–1663) and his heirs. In 1639, Gardiner purchased the island that bears his name on the east end from the Montaukette for "one large dog, one gun, some powder and shot, some rum and several blankets, worth in all about Five Pounds sterling." The sale of and annual quit claim for West Beach commenced on June 10, 1658, for a considerable sum of money and included all of the beach between a point opposite Canoe Point and the Brookhaven town line. The agreement also had stipulations for the sachem and his heirs to receive perpetual yearly payments of 25 shillings every October, along with rights to beached whales to remain with him and the Shinnecock. (EHL.)

122

Southampton, L. I.

On the Bathing Beach

In June 1910, the Southampton Bathing Association was incorporated "to establish and conduct a bathing pavilion." The c. 1911 postcard above shows the public beach and pavilion in the vicinity of Gin Lane and south of Agawam Lake. The Bathing Corporation of Southampton ("The Beach Club") acquired the property in 1923, and in 1927, the *East Hampton Star* announced construction of new amenities, including an expanded Spanish-style pavilion, saltwater pool, showers, and additional bathhouses. The c. 1935 postcard below shows a view of the beach, which became private in 1939. *Long Island Gazetteer: A Guide to Historic Places* (1939), compiled by Arthur R. Macoskey, stated Southampton was the "Newport of Long Island" with "a magnificent beach, beautiful and palatial residences, and the hotel, club and social life of the neighborhood attract well-known families." (Both, PC.)

SOUTHAMPTON BATHING BEACH AND PAVILION, SOUTHAMPTON, LONG ISLAND, N. Y.

The High Dunes East   Water Mill Shore, Long Island, N. Y.

Flying Point Beach is located in the hamlet of Water Mill. The Burnett family gifted the land to the Town of Southampton in 1952. The Burnetts acquired property here in 1674 when the area was called Cormorant Poynt. During Prohibition (1920–1933), historical sources suggest Long Island residents purchased alcohol from Canadian and Caribbean ships in close proximity to this beach. (PC.)

The Jagger family owned the Cedar Beach Club or House (later Hotel) and 10-cottage complex on Moriches Bay in Westhampton. In 1969, the Westhampton Yacht Squadron acquired the main building. It was transported in sections on barges to Remsenburg and reassembled to serve as the squadron's clubhouse. Pictured from left to right in 1925 are a very attentive dog, Mary Townsend Jagger, Archer W. Jagger Jr., and Helen Jagger. (WBHS.)

West Beach Bathing Pavilion   Westhampton Beach, Long Island, N. Y.

Several beachgoers are pictured on this postcard relaxing on the sand at the swanky West Beach Bathing Pavilion in Westhampton Beach, between Moriches Bay and the Atlantic Ocean, where Jessup Lane and Dune Road meet. This area was particularly devastated by a direct hit from the Great New England Hurricane in 1938. The Swordfish Club rebuilt on the grounds and opened in June 1940. (WBHS.)

Rustic shade arbors were fabricated on many east end beaches, including in Westhampton Beach. Arbors typically had posts made from oak saplings and roofs comprised of scrub oak branches and thatch. These covered shelters provided relief from the sun and served as gathering spots for conversing, picnicking, and playing games. (WBHS.)

Long Island–born poet Walt Whitman (1819–1892) was inspired by landscapes and geography throughout his lifetime, including at Montauk, Orient, Shelter Island, and New York City. His poem "Starting from Paumanok," titled after an original name Native Americans gave Long Island, was first published in the *New York Herald* on February 29, 1888, and later in the 1891 final edition of *Leaves of Grass*. Whitman wrote "Starting from Paumanok" toward the end of his life. The poem is a lasting tribute to Long Island, which captures the duality and beauty of its shorelines. "Sea-beauty! stretch'd and basking! / One side thy inland ocean laving, broad, / with copious commerce, steamers, sails, / And one the Atlantic's wind caressing, fierce / or gentle—with mighty hulls dark-gliding / in the distance: / Isle of sweet drinking-water— healthy air / and soil!—isle of the earth and brine!" (PC.)

BIBLIOGRAPHY

Armbruster, Eugene L. *Landmarks on the Montauk Highway and Long Island Directory with Map.* Brooklyn, NY: E.L. Armbruster, 1925.

Blakelock, Chester R. *History of the Long Island State Parks.* Amityville, NY: Long Island Forum (permission of the Lewis Historical Publishing Co.), 1959.

Caro, Robert A. *The Power Broker: Robert Moses and the Fall of New York.* New York, NY: Vintage Books, 1975.

Corbin, Alain. *The Lure of the Sea: The Discovery of the Seaside in the Western World, 1750–1840.* Berkeley, CA: University of California Press, 1994.

Gabriel, Ralph Henry. *The Evolution of Long Island: A Story of Land and Sea.* New Haven, CT: Yale University Press, 1921.

Hanc, John. *Jones Beach: An Illustrated History.* Guilford, CT: Globe Pequot Press, 2007.

Harrison, Helen A., and Constance A. Denne. *Hamptons Bohemia: Two Centuries of Artists and Writers on the Beach.* San Francisco, CA: Chronicle Books, 2002.

Hyde, E.B. *Real Estate Reference Map of Nassau County, Long Island.* New York, NY: E. Belcher Hyde, 1927.

Jones Beach State Park. New York, NY: Long Island State Park Commission, 1933.

Koppelman, Lee. *The Urban Sea: Long Island Sound.* New York, NY: Praeger Publishers, 1976.

Lencek, Lena, and Gideon Bosker. *The Beach: The History of Paradise on Earth.* New York, NY: Viking, 1998.

Lynch, Patrick J. *A Field Guide to Long Island Sound: Coastal Habitats, Plant Life, Fish, Seabirds, Marine Mammals, and Other Wildlife.* New Haven, CT: Yale University Press, 2017.

Prochaska, David, and Jordana Mendelson. *Postcards: Ephemeral Histories of Modernity.* University Park, PA: Pennsylvania State University Press, 2010.

Regional Survey of New York and its Environs. New York, NY: Regional Plan of New York and Its Environs, 1927–1931.

Tanski, Jay. *Long Island's Dynamic South Shore: A Primer on the Forces and Trends Shaping Our Coast.* Stony Brook, NY: Stony Brook University, New York Sea Grant Extension Program, 2007.

Tooker, William Wallace. *The Indian Place-Names on Long Island and Islands Adjacent, with Their Probable Significations.* New York, NY: G.P. Putnam's Sons, 1911.

DISCOVER THOUSANDS OF LOCAL HISTORY BOOKS FEATURING MILLIONS OF VINTAGE IMAGES

Arcadia Publishing, the leading local history publisher in the United States, is committed to making history accessible and meaningful through publishing books that celebrate and preserve the heritage of America's people and places.

Find more books like this at
www.arcadiapublishing.com

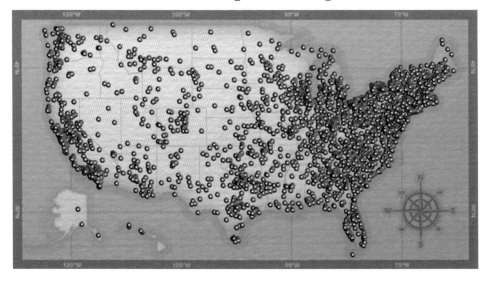

Search for your hometown history, your old stomping grounds, and even your favorite sports team.